Will You Take Me Home?

Will You Take Me Home?

The brave rescue dog from the puppy
farm who became a movie star

Julie Tottman

sphere

SPHERE

First published in Great Britain in 2020 by Sphere

1 3 5 7 9 10 8 6 4 2

A CIP catalogue record for this book is available from the British Library.

ISBN 978-0-7515-8009-9

Typeset in Goudy by M Rules
Printed and bound in Great Britain by Clays Ltd, Elcograf S.p.A.

Papers used by Sphere are from well-managed forests
and other responsible sources.

MIX
Paper from
responsible sources
FSC® C104740

Sphere
An imprint of
Little, Brown Book Group
Carmelite House
50 Victoria Embankment
London EC4Y 0DZ

An Hachette UK Company
www.hachette.co.uk

www.littlebrown.co.uk

Contents

Prologue

Out of the Darkness

It was the darkness that was the worst. In the pitch black of the barn, all you could hear were the whimpers of the other dogs. The smell was overwhelming; a nasty, fetid stench which told of the dirt and disease that bound us together in misery. In the blackness, you could make out the gleaming eyes of my cell mates as they clambered over each other in search of somewhere dry to settle down and sleep. They would never find it in this filthy hellhole.

I had never known any different, but something told me this was not a life any dog should lead. A Yorkshire terrier like me should be curled up on someone's lap, not shivering in a damp and dirty prison. It was no place to raise babies, but I had a litter of eight helpless puppies by my side. Just feeling them squirm against me, their soft new fur warm and comforting, was enough to make my heart feel like it might burst with devotion. I knew I could endure anything as long as I had them.

There were other dogs in the barn with puppies too, all doing what they could to survive. We would all lay down our lives for our babies but each of us lived in constant fear that they would one day be wrenched away. It had happened before, you see. I could hardly bear to remember it, but I had reared litters many times – only to have them cruelly stolen from me before they were old enough to leave. This was my sixth litter. My heart broke as I remembered the ones who had come

2

before. Taken too soon, they had squealed with fear and anguish as we were separated. Where were they now?

I wished I could take my babies out into the sunlight. We got a glimpse of it every morning, when a man in heavy boots would heave open the barn door and toss measly amounts of food directly onto the dirty floor of our steel-barred cages. Every morning I'd wag my tail tentatively. Maybe today he would reach down and pat my head? Or unlatch my cage door and lead us out into the fresh air? But he never did. He would simply slam the door shut behind him.

Plunged back into the dark, it was hard to know when the day was over and when night began. It made no difference really. The discomfort was as intense whatever time it was. I could feel the mites crawling through my itchy ears while my body burned from whatever painful skin condition I had developed. My stomach churned but going to the loo felt like wrenching out my insides.

Every bit of me ached. I couldn't keep myself clean, and I shivered from the cold caused by my own dampness.

Some days I could feel my strength ebbing away. There were so many of us in the barn, and many of the dogs were very sick – you could smell it on them, like decay. One had gone blind; another could no longer stand up. But I couldn't give in, I had to be strong for my babies. I looked down at them and counted eight little bodies. The littlest one was worryingly weak. He couldn't keep his head up to suckle, and I could feel his heartbeat slowing as I frantically licked his tiny body. *Stay strong, little one!* I willed him. I had to keep him alive.

The puppies and I fell into a fitful sleep. I dreamed I was outside in a sunlit meadow, roaming free while my babies played happily beside me. Then there was a bang and I woke with a start. Was it feeding time already? Sunlight streamed in through the door, illuminating the ominous figure of the farmer. He was with a younger man today and – oh God – they were both holding crates. Suddenly I was on high alert, throwing my body across my pups. It was then that I realised in horror that the little one was stone cold. He'd left me already.

I was howling with grief by the time the younger man reached my pen. He unlatched the cage door and reached down towards my remaining puppies. Not this time! I bared my little teeth and barked and barked, but it only prompted him to aim a powerful kick at my abdomen. I felt the wind rush out of me as I was thrown against the wall. By the time I had staggered back to my feet it was too late. Every last baby was gone – they had even taken the tiny little corpse.

'How many then, Jack?' I heard the farmer ask the other man.

'I've counted thirty-three,' came the reply.

'Should be quite the payday! Couple of casualties, though: two dead and one at death's door.'

'Chuck the dead ones on the bonfire,' said the farmer. The door slammed shut behind them.

The howls of pain echoing through the barn told me I was not the only mother who had been robbed of her children that day. Our little ones weren't ready – they were still far too young to fend for themselves. Instinct told me they should have stayed with me for at least another two weeks. I could only imagine the terror my poor puppies must be feeling now, and I thought I would go mad with the agony of it all. I scrabbled desperately at the bars of my cage, but it was no use. I was trapped here for ever. When would this awful cycle end? I feared I may not survive the physical and emotional toll of raising and losing yet another litter.

Some time later – days or months, I couldn't be sure – the barn door opened at a different time from normal. I barely bothered to look up – what could it mean except more suffering? Then I heard voices I didn't recognise. I hurried to the edge of my pen and put my paws on the bars. I could see several pairs of feet, and one of them was heading my way.

'Oh heavens! How could anyone do such awful things to defenceless animals?' I heard someone say. I lifted my head and saw a blond-haired woman peering into my pen. Everything inside me told me not to trust her, to stay well back in case she hurt me like all the other humans had done. But I couldn't help it. Feebly, I wagged my tail. Maybe she was different from the others. Maybe she would give me the kindness I had longed for all my life.

'Look at the state of you,' she said as she reached towards me. 'Let's get you out of here. You're safe now.'

She scooped me up and held me against her chest. I had no idea where she was taking me or what it all meant. But the warmth of her body and the gentleness of her touch felt like something I could trust. She turned and walked towards the open door and the beckoning sunlight.

Exhausted, I slumped my head against her chest and allowed sleep to carry me away. Was I really safe at last?

Chapter One

Starting from Scratch

I flung open the windows of my little cottage and breathed in the fresh spring air. It was one of those glorious bright blue mornings where the scent of blossom hangs tantalisingly on the breeze. I could hear the lambs in the next-door farm bleating gently and see a cheerful clutch of daffodils swaying in the garden. The day felt full of possibility.

Grabbing my cup of tea, I wandered out into the pretty garden, keen to make the most of a morning which heralded the return of warm weather after the gloom of winter. I still hadn't got over the novelty of perching on my tumbledown wall and taking stock while my boxers, George and Ginelli, sniffed around the flower beds and songbirds chirruped in the trees. It was a far cry from the cramped little patio of my old flat, where the only morning chorus you heard was the honking horns of traffic and distant trains whizzing by.

The nineteenth-century cottage, with its ivy-clad walls, cosy nooks and stone-flagged floors, was still quite new to me, as I had only moved in a month ago. But I was in love with it already. The noise and pollution of London felt like a distant memory, and I could see how much the boxers, as well as my white poodle Gypsy and Lala the Dalmatian, were enjoying being country dogs.

'Not a bad way to start the day, is it?' I asked Gypsy, the princess of the pack, who liked to hop up on the wall next to me while I sipped my tea.

I had always planned to move out of the city

eventually but it was still a big step to leave behind Harrow, the suburb where I'd spent most of my life, and start a new chapter out in the countryside. In the end, the move had been for practical reasons. My job training animals for films was growing ever busier and it made sense for me to be closer to Shepperton and Pinewood studios, where I did most of my work, rather than doing battle with the M25 every morning. Days on set could be long – sometimes as much as twelve hours a day – so I was grateful for the quicker commute.

The cottage was perfect, with three bedrooms, a snug living room and a big, bright kitchen with an Aga – and a lovely warm spot on the flagstone floor in front of it where the dogs could curl up. As soon as I moved in, I had painted all the walls in cheerful yellows and peaches, and hung pretty floral curtains at the windows.

I didn't know a soul in the village I'd moved to – Long Marston in Hertfordshire – but it didn't matter because it already felt like home. I loved wandering its winding lanes lined with hedgerows and spotting red kites circling overhead, looking for food. I had my dogs, as well as my two cats, Jazz and Sky, for company. The village had a couple of welcoming pubs and a small shop, and with so much natural beauty on the doorstep I didn't feel I needed anything else.

Gulping a mouthful of tea and feeling the sun warm my cheeks, I still couldn't believe it had taken me so long to take the plunge. As a born and bred city girl, I thought I would miss being able to go and see any film I wanted at any time of day or night, or to choose from about fifty takeaway options on a lazy Friday evening. But I couldn't miss any of it less. The quiet, the cleanliness of the air, the miles of uninterrupted fields over which I romped with my dogs – it all made perfect sense. It felt like the beginning of a whole new life.

This year – 2003 – was a fresh start for me in more ways than one. Having worked for the legendary Hollywood trainer Gary Gero for the last few years, I was now striking out on my own. Gary had given me my first big break back in 1995, when he had hired me as the head dog trainer on *101 Dalmatians*. Then I had gone on to train animals for the Harry Potter films, working alongside his US-based team. For those movies we had trained about 250 animals in total, from a slobbery mastiff who played Hagrid's dog Fang to some very dim-witted owls who proved quite a challenge. I smiled guiltily as I remembered one of the owls grabbing not the letter prop it was meant to, but the director's important production notes and swooping off without a backward glance as we desperately tried to catch her.

Despite a few mishaps with the owls, Gary must have been impressed. Now that the second Potter movie, *Harry Potter and the Chamber of Secrets*, was out of the way, he had appointed me director of a new UK arm of his company, Birds & Animals. The idea was that I would run it, becoming increasingly independent of the US sister company as time went on. Filming Potter had been a whirl-wind, but taking charge of my own branch of the business was going to be a challenge in its own right. I was so proud that Gary had put his faith in me and determined not to let him down.

Now was the chance to prove myself, because I had just secured the first job for Birds & Animals UK. We had been contracted to supply and train a dog for a new teen movie called *What a Girl Wants*. It was an American production, but it was mainly set in Britain, so most of the film-ing would take place over here. The teen star Amanda Bynes was set to play an American girl who discovers her long-lost dad is an aristocratic British politician, played by Colin Firth. A quest to reconnect with her dad lands Amanda's character in the midst of British high society – and brings her face to face with the royal family. The script called for a Yorkshire terrier who would play a dog belonging to Sylvia Syms's character, Princess Charlotte, a little diva of a thing who bonds with

Amanda Bynes, endearing her to the aristocrats. It would be my job to cast and train the dog.

I knew I had to enjoy the peace of the garden while I could, because I had a busy few months ahead of me. I was on my own now and it was down to me to make it work. The search for a new canine star was about to begin.

Chapter Two

Casting Call

Right on cue, the phone rang from the kitchen. I hurried inside, knowing it would be Jo Vaughan, a fellow trainer who had come on board the new company.

'All right, Jules?' came Jo's familiar voice down the line. 'What are we thinking about this Yorkie, then?'

I smiled. Jo wasn't one for much of a preamble, she was too no-nonsense for that. It was one of the things I loved about her. We had been working together for four years, since we first hit it off on the set of *102 Dalmatians* in 1999. Jo had been on the team of puppy trainers Gary had hired for that film, and from day one we just clicked. Her diligence and unflappable nature meant she stood out from the rest. I only found out later that it was her first time working with dogs, having previously trained sea lions for shows at a safari park. You would never have guessed when you saw how natural she was around the puppies.

Jo and I quickly learned that we train and think in a very similar way. Like me, she puts the happiness of the animal at the centre of everything she does and never compromises when it comes to making training fun and nurturing. Over the years we had become not just colleagues but firm friends, and one of the reasons I had ended up in this part of Hertfordshire was because she lived not far away. Now that we were striking out from the US business, Jo and I were working more closely together than ever. Finding myself faced with business decisions on a daily basis, I relied on her support and good judgement, and I already saw her as my right-hand woman. Just last night we had been texting about *What a Girl Wants*, and Jo had promised to help me find the perfect dog.

'I haven't worked with any Yorkshire terriers before, but what I do know is that we've got to get it right,' I told her now, scratching Gypsy behind the ears as I spoke. I knew that Yorkies were known to be energetic and feisty, which would be great for training, but also that some can have a tendency to be a bit snappy or yappy.

'The director told me he wants a dog with proper star quality: "a scene-stealer" was how he put it.' I didn't need to add that as our first job as a solo outfit, there was a lot riding on this one.

'Well, it could be our lucky day,' said Jo. 'I've just been in touch with an old contact of mine, who trained the Yorkie in that bank advert – you know, the one that was everywhere about a year ago? The dog is still working and knows all the basics already, apparently. Could be just what we need.'

It did indeed sound almost too good to be true. But still I hesitated. *What a Girl Wants* was an opportunity for me to set out my stall and put into practice the values I hold dear. My very first dog when I was a child had been a rescue, and I wanted to continue that legacy. I've therefore always tried to use rescue dogs in films whenever I can because I truly believe that every animal deserves a second chance. And there are so many wonderful animals languishing in rescue centres that it would be a waste not to look there as a first port of call when embarking on a new project. These animals are literally on the scrap heap after years of cruelty or neglect, and I know I can give them the lovely life they so desperately deserve. Over the years I've taken in animals who have been starved, beaten, abandoned and just plain unloved. There have been cats so dirty there are maggots burrowing through their skin and dogs who don't know what it's like to be let loose to run free. The world had given up on these animals as lost causes – in some cases, they would have been put to sleep if I hadn't plucked them from their rescue centre. Given that second chance at life, they all went on to repay me a thousand times over with their talent for training and enormous capacity for love.

But on the other hand, filming started in just three months' time, and we didn't have any other leads. I had been ringing round my usual contacts at rescue centres and dog charities to see if they had any Yorkies who would fit the bill, but so far I had drawn a blank. So the Yorkshire terrier from the bank advert could be the perfect solution.

'Sounds great, Jo,' I said. 'Can you email me over a video of the dog being put through his paces?'

'Doing it now,' she replied, and hung up.

I opened up my laptop and logged on to my email. As I waited for Jo's video to pop through,

I scrolled idly through the BBC News website. Then something caught my eye which changed everything. Perhaps I would be able to cast a rescue dog after all.

Chapter Three

A Twist of Fate

'Dozens of dogs kept in shocking conditions at illegal puppy farm' read the headline.

Already feeling sick at the thought of the cruelty the dogs must have endured, I clicked on the link. The story was about a raid on a farm near Swansea where animal inspectors found starving and dying dogs being held in sheds and barns while the unscrupulous owners made tens of thousands of pounds from selling puppies online.

The father and son who ran the awful enterprise

posed as caring family sellers, but in reality their dogs were little more than breeding machines. More than fifty dogs had been removed from their filthy barns but they were so poorly cared for that two had already had to be put to sleep. Tipped off that they were about to be raided, the breeders had fled – and police were now hunting them so they could be brought to justice for the horrors they had inflicted.

I scrolled open-mouthed through pictures of the hellish pens where emaciated dogs cowered with their puppies, surrounded by faeces. The article reported how most of the dogs had painful skin conditions, infections and sores but had barely seen daylight, let alone a vet. Animal cruelty is nothing new, but every time I'm confronted with it I'm still astounded by how humans can treat defenceless creatures in such a way.

'These poor dogs,' I murmured, half to myself and half to Ginelli, my handsome red boxer who had followed me in from the garden. Ginelli was also a rescue dog, and had been nervous around humans when I got him, but like George, a white boxer with a big brown patch over one eye who had been taken to a boarding kennels by an owner who clearly didn't want him, then just never picked up, he had responded with joy to the training I gave him. Both dogs went on to work successfully in films and adverts, and they were also wonderful pets – George was so gentle and sweet despite the neglect he had experienced, and Ginelli had this madcap, adventurous spirit which never failed to make me laugh. They were living proof that no matter what an animal's past, the right love and care can give them a bright future.

I could only hope that the dogs rescued from the puppy farm would get the new life they deserved. Right at the end of the piece, it mentioned that the rescued dogs had been temporarily placed in a local rehoming centre, which was appealing for potential new owners to come forward.

'What do you think, then?' I asked Ginelli, who had stationed himself by my side and was peering at the computer screen, trying to see what I was transfixed by. 'What are the chances they have a Yorkshire terrier?'

Ginelli sighed and settled himself at my feet as I hammered the name of the rescue centre into the search engine. I was dialling their number before the page had even properly loaded. I knew it was a long shot, but it had to be worth a try.

The woman who answered the phone with a soft Welsh accent told me they had been over-whelmed with offers of new homes ever since the story went live.

'We do have a couple of dogs still looking for a place, though,' she went on. 'Some of the older bitches – they've been bred until they're almost broken. They are the poorliest of the lot and it's made it harder for us to find someone to take them on.'

My heart broke at the thought of these pitiful creatures who were exploited for profit and would undoubtedly have been dumped as soon as they outlived their usefulness. The Kennel Club recommends that dogs only have up to four litters in their lifetime and most vets advise resting the mothers between cycles. But on puppy farms the dogs are bred every time they are in season – every six months – and the only limit to how many litters they have is how many they can produce before they drop dead.

'Can I ask what breeds the remaining dogs are?' I asked, barely daring to hope.

'Yes, there's a couple of schnauzers, but someone is coming to look at them this afternoon,' the woman replied, 'and there's a Yorkshire terrier too.'

I couldn't believe it. My head was spinning as I hung up, promising I'd be there to see the Yorkie as soon as I could. I clicked back onto my email and saw that the video from Jo had dropped in. Not even bothering to watch it, I typed out a reply. 'Thanks for finding this but let's pause for now. Another Yorkie has come up. Do you mind

26

watching my dogs today? Am driving to Wales – will explain later.'

Jo replied within minutes – she had a key to the cottage and was happy to come and take the dogs out. 'Intrigued to hear what you're up to this time . . .' she added.

I was out of the door and into the driving seat of my battered Mitsubishi Shogun in ten minutes flat, glancing quickly at the road atlas so I knew where I was going. What were the chances of the last remaining dog from the puppy farm being a Yorkie – just when I needed one? There was no other word for it: this had to be fate.

Chapter Four

To the Rescue

On the four-hour drive to Wales, all I could think about was those poor dogs, locked in the dark on the puppy farm. Images of the squalid conditions they'd been kept in raced through my mind, and I could feel the anger against the people who did this building inside me.

All puppy farmers care about is profit. And they don't care how much their animals suffer as a result. If all you are concerned about is your bottom line, then basic health measures like immunisation and worming go out of the window. This means the dogs will probably suffer from preventable infectious diseases and painful skin, eye or ear conditions. They will usually have a shorter life span too.

Puppy-farm dogs are usually fed just enough to keep them alive and kept in conditions you wouldn't wish on your worst enemy. With so many dogs crammed together, disease thrives. Unscrupulous to the last, the breeders don't care if they are interbreeding brother and sister dogs, creating more chronic health problems for their offspring. Then the puppies are separated from their mothers far earlier than the recommended eight weeks, because the breeders are so eager to cash in as quickly as possible.

But these people are clever. When prospective buyers come to view the pups they certainly wouldn't be shown to the nasty barns where they are really kept. Instead, puppy farmers pose as small-time family breeders, making it look like the puppies have been reared in a safe, clean environment. They might even have a healthy dog as a fake mum because they know the advice to buyers is to always see puppies with their mother. Unsuspecting customers then hand over hundreds of pounds for a puppy which is potentially very sick, or even dying. It's an enormous problem, too – while it is impossible to say for certain, one estimate says up to four hundred thousand farmed puppies are sold in the UK every year.

As far as I'm concerned, puppy farms are factories of evil. No dog should be made to live like that. I felt so relieved that the Welsh farm had been busted, but so sad for the animals which had endured it for so long.

I was pretty sure I would be unable to resist taking the Yorkshire terrier home with me, even if she would never make it as a movie dog. How could I leave her behind after what she had been through? While I believe any animal can be trained, I don't think they are all cut out for film sets, which can be demanding places.

Lala was one dog who didn't quite make it. I had taken her on in the hope she would star in *102 Dalmatians*, but no matter how much we trained she could never keep her attention on the task in hand. She was such a strong-willed girl that I knew she was wasn't right for the film, but also that she needed an experienced owner who could cope with her boisterous personality. That's why I kept her – a decision I have never regretted. She had settled into being a wonderful pet and companion to my other dogs.

As in the case of Lala, I would never take an animal on set unless I was absolutely confident they would be able to deal with the conditions. A dog like this Yorkie, who had probably had little to no human contact throughout her miserable life, might struggle. I doubted she had ever been on a collar and lead, and the chances of serious behavioural issues were high.

It would have been far simpler to just stick with the dog from the bank advert that Jo had found, who was already used to being on set and learning commands. But there was something about the timing of all this that made me determined to check out the dog from the puppy farm before making that decision. My gut instinct told me it was meant to be.

I wouldn't know for sure just by looking at the Yorkie today, however. You can rarely tell what a dog's real personality is like until you get them in a relaxed home environment. A good dog for a film set has loads of energy, a bold nature and a good appetite. They might be a little bit naughty, but that can be a good thing – those sorts of dogs love the mental stimulation training brings. As long as they are friendly and outgoing, and greedy enough to bribe with treats, you can work from there.

In the past, I had found all these attributes in the most unlikely of places. Rescue dogs especially can have an extraordinary desire to please, as if they are grateful for their new life. So I wasn't writing off the puppy-farm Yorkie just yet.

I was so caught up in my thoughts that I almost missed the turning to the rescue centre, a squat grey building on the outskirts of Swansea. Finally pulling into the car park, I found the woman I'd spoken to on the phone, Carys, waiting for me outside.

'I can't believe you've come so far!' she greeted me. 'Honestly, we've been blown away by the response of the public to this story. It just goes to show there are still good people out there.'

'What a shame there's still some bad ones who would do this in the first place,' I replied, and she nodded grimly.

On the phone, I had explained to Carys what I do and why I was so keen to see the Yorkshire terrier. She was intrigued but I could hear the doubt in her voice as she tried to manage my expectations, telling me the little dog was lucky to be alive. I had reassured her I was only interested in making the pup happy again – whether through training or not.

'Let me introduce you to our little Yorkie,' she said now, leading me through a set of glass double doors into the rescue centre. 'But I have to warn you: she's an upsetting sight. How that dog has endured the things she has, we'll never know.'

I tried to keep the nervousness from my face. Yes, I had rescued plenty of animals – but not a dog from a puppy farm. I knew the Yorkie would have all sorts of issues I had never dealt with before, and I had to hope I would be able to give her the love and care she deserved. Was I up to the challenge, with everything else I had on my plate? It was time to find out.

Chapter Five

Puppy Love at First Sight

I always find rescue centres difficult places – I just want to take each and every one of the animals home with me. This one was no exception.

Carys, a motherly woman in her late fifties who emanated a peaceful kindness, led me down a noisy corridor lined with dogs who pushed their little faces against the bars of their enclosures. As usual, there were lots of Staffies and lurchers, who seem to end up in rescue centres more than any other kind of dog. Looking into their pleading eyes, I hoped they would soon find loving for-ever homes.

I could see that the dogs here were being well cared for by Carys and her team, who seemed as dedicated as I was to giving deserving creatures another chance at happiness. She was chatting away to me about the dogs from the puppy farm, who had been brought in last week by animal inspectors. We passed the schnauzers she had mentioned on the phone, who were skinny and subdued. As well as these and the Yorkies, inspectors had also found Cavalier King Charles spaniels, bichon frises and French bulldogs – all popular breeds which would be easy for the puppy farmers to sell for great profit.

Carys told me that some of the sickest dogs were still receiving round-the-clock treatment at the vet's, and it was uncertain if they would survive. 'The authorities are getting better at raiding these farms, but I think the problem is getting worse,' she said. 'It's because it's not just pet shops we have to contend with now, it's internet sellers too.'

As we talked, I peered into the kennels, which were clean and bright. There were about thirty enclosures, each with a large indoor area, probably about 3 metres by 2 metres, scattered with plenty of toys, and with cosy, cushion-lined beds set up. At the back, the kennels opened up into an outdoor run where the dogs could play. I thought how different it must feel for the dogs from the puppy farm, who had spent their whole life crammed into tiny pens in the dark.

We reached the final kennel, spacious and sunlit, and Carys unlatched the door, whistling gently to the dog within. With a little coaxing, a Yorkshire terrier emerged from a crate they had set up for her to hide in, and padded shyly towards us.

Even though I had been preparing myself for the worst, I was shocked by the state of the creature before me. She was one of the saddest sights I had ever seen. Her little body was covered in a thick layer of mange, her matted hair was falling out and her ears looked painfully inflamed and crusty. I immediately clocked her sagging belly, a tell-tale sign that she had been bred and bred. Right now, she certainly didn't look like a dog who could pass for the pet of a princess.

'The vet says she has a fair few issues,' Carys confirmed. 'We reckon she's probably about five years old but, at a guess, she's already had six litters of puppies. It's criminal – her body didn't have a chance of recovering.'

'Did the animal inspectors find any puppies with her when they raided the place?' I asked, reaching out my hand towards the little dog so she could have a sniff.

Carys shook her head. 'But she's definitely had some recently,' she added. 'We think she's still pining for them now.'

After suffering all of that, I would understand why a dog like this would be terrified of humans, and show aggression or fear when faced with a new one. And yet the little Yorkie looked up at me with her big brown eyes, and there was something trusting about the way she held my gaze.

Standing only about seven inches tall, she was small for her breed. Although her coat was in a terrible condition I could tell it was meant to be a rich, tawny auburn. She wagged her tail tentatively and her mouth parted ever so slightly, making it look like she was smiling. I felt my heart lurch.

'She's a gorgeous little thing really,' Carys went on. 'Look how friendly she is – the animal inspectors said she was one of the few who went with them with no fuss at all.'

I crouched down so I was at the same level as the Yorkie. 'Hello, gorgeous girl,' I said to her, and her nose twitched. I could see her daring herself to be brave, and then she took one small, nervous step towards me. Carefully, I reached behind her ears and gave her a gentle stroke. Her gaze never faltered even though her weak little body trembled. I knew immediately that this was one special animal.

At moments like this I always think that dogs are simply too good for us humans, that we don't deserve them. The Yorkie had been abused in the worst possible way and yet here she was, willing to love and trust again, despite being so often betrayed. I had no idea whether she would be right for *What a Girl Wants*. But I knew for certain she was coming home with me.

Chapter Six

Homeward Bound

'It sounds like she's going to have a wonderful new life,' Carys told me as I signed the necessary paperwork. We had been talking about how my cottage was set up – with the dogs having the run of the house, beds by the warm Aga and a flap to get out into the back garden whenever they wanted. Carys thought it would be good for the Yorkie to be around other dogs, as she was used to living with others. Most importantly, Carys was reassured that I had lots of experience with rescue animals, so I knew how much patience is required.

When everything was rubber-stamped, Carys helped me pack the Yorkie into my car. It had been specially adapted with cage bars so I could safely carry several animals at once in separate crates. Each travelling pen was lined with a comfy bed and cuddly toys to keep the dogs happy during the journey. Carys fetched a pink blanket, which had been in the Yorkie's kennel bed, to travel with her.

As I picked her up to tuck her into the crate, I could feel the Yorkie's birdlike skeleton and her fluttering heartbeat, which told me she might be more nervous than she let on. 'Don't worry, pup,' I whispered to her. 'You're going to be so happy in your new home. I'll make sure of it.'

It was a long drive back to Long Marston, especially as we had to stop so often for the Yorkie to go to the loo. She was pooping blood and clearly had a very upset stomach – yet another sign of the unhygienic conditions she'd been kept in, where tummy bugs spread like wildfire.

'What a pickle you're in!' I told her as she squatted on the verge outside yet another service station. 'Just as well I brought plenty of poo bags!' By our fifth stop, the name Pickles had stuck.

'What do you think – will Pickles do?' I asked her as we turned back onto the motorway. In the rear-view mirror I could see her little head through the bars of her crate, and she was watching me with a look of amused curiosity. I kept chatting away to her and she would turn her head this way and that, like she was really listening. Already I was amazed by how little seemed to faze her.

It was dark by the time we got back to the cottage. When I'm away from home for more than a couple of hours – whether it's on a film set or on a rescue mission – I always get Jo or one of the other animal handlers I work with to watch the dogs. I could tell Jo had dropped the dogs back already, as there was a welcoming glow coming from the kitchen window, where she had left the light on.

I bundled Pickles up in my jacket to carry her inside. The other dogs bounded over to have a good sniff of the exciting new arrival I was cradling in my arms. Gypsy took one look and stalked off – she was never too happy about anything that would mean she was no longer centre of attention. I made a mental note to give her lots of cuddles this evening so she knew she was just as loved as ever.

As the other dogs gave Pickles the once-over, I thought she might panic, but she merely blinked at them. Lala bounded off to fetch her favourite toy, a display which Pickles watched with bewilderment. 'I don't think she's ready to play just yet, Lala,' I laughed.

I carried Pickles to the blue-tiled bathroom and ran her a bath. Some dogs hate getting washed, but

Pickles made contented little noises as I massaged her all over with doggy shampoo. I think it must have given her some temporary relief from her painful skin condition.

'You'll have to see the vet first thing tomorrow,' I murmured to her as I lifted her out of the bath and started trying to gently tease out the tangles in her coat with a comb. 'I think we're going to need some more heavy-duty shampoo – and some medicine too.'

But first I wanted Pickles to get some rest. Even though it was spring there was still a slight chill in the air and I didn't want her to be cold for even a moment. So I laid a fire in the living room and busied myself building her a little nest of blankets. She stood and watched me calmly, and I could sense her mind whirring as she took in her new surroundings.

When I was done, I lifted her gently onto the blankets and retreated to my squashy red sofa, keen to give her some space. I was keenly aware that this might be overwhelming for a dog who had spent her entire life in a dark barn with little human contact.

Pickles sat on the blankets with her back perfectly straight, then turned around to look at me. For a second she stared at me, then trotted over and sat right at my feet, looking up at me with those soulful brown eyes.

'Oh – you want to come and sit up here, do you?' I could hardly believe how friendly she was; she already seemed to have decided I could be trusted. She didn't even flinch as I reached down and picked her up, scooping her onto my lap. She snuggled into my chest and at last, for the first time since we'd come face to face, she seemed to settle. As the fire flickered I felt her breathing slow down, and I knew she'd fallen asleep.

Pickles was physically very ill, but the sweetest little soul clearly resided inside. I knew already that there was something special about her.

Only time would tell if I would be able to get her

well enough to start training, or how she would respond when I did. But in that moment I didn't care. All that mattered was that Pickles was here with me – and the horrors of her past were over.

Chapter Seven

Road to Recovery

That night I tossed and turned, unable to sleep because I was so worried about the little terrier downstairs. Was she frightened to be so far away from everything she knew? Was she still missing her babies? So many questions raced through my head, and I knew there was a lot of hard work ahead of me.

When I went downstairs in the morning, it seemed Pickles had not endured a sleepless night herself. She looked remarkably bright eyed and well rested, although in the cold light of the morning her mangy skin looked even worse than it did last night. She had also made quite a mess in the kitchen. Her stomach was clearly still very dodgy and, as a breeding dog, she had never been housetrained.

'Just as well the floor is wipe-clean,' I joked to her as I cleared it all up. 'I'm going to let you off because you're so poorly, but toilet training is definitely top of your to-do list.' Gypsy looked at me knowingly – if a dog could roll her eyes, she would be doing so.

After I fed the other dogs, I made Pickles a small breakfast of some chicken and rice, hoping it would start to calm down her digestive system. Vets recommend this meal for pups with diarrhoea as it is bland but nutritious and works to soothe an upset tummy. I'd had enough poorly dogs over the years that I was a dab hand at boiling the chicken breast and cooking the rice in the broth.

When I set the meal in front of Pickles she

picked at it gingerly, but at least she was eating. I desperately needed to get her strength up but that would be a challenge if the food was going straight through her.

Keeping one eye on her, I dialled the vet's number and booked an appointment for later that morning.

Next, I tapped in Jo's familiar number. 'Let me guess,' she answered. 'There was some poor helpless stray on the other side of the country you simply had to rescue, and now we're going to be up against it trying to get ready for the film on time.' I grinned. She knew me so well. And I knew her well enough to know that she would have done exactly the same.

As I filled Jo in on Pickles's story, I heard her take a sharp intake of breath when I described the horrible conditions the dogs had been kept in. Jo detested animal cruelty too – it's why she had so many rescues of her own. When I had finished, there was a pause. Then she said: 'That dog deserves all the love and care in the world, Julie. The film can wait – just get her well.'

I had known Jo would understand – for her, like me, training and loving animals is a way of life, not just a job. But there were still a lot of question marks over Pickles. Jo and I agreed that she would go and see the Yorkie from the bank advert, so we could have a back-up just in case. 'But just so you know, I'm rooting for Pickles,' she told me. My heart swelled. I was too.

By now Pickles had finished her breakfast and, as expected, it had come straight back out again. The poor thing was obviously in serious discomfort. 'What are we going to do with you?' I asked her, pulling her onto my knee after I had cleaned her up, an act of affection she accepted without question. Despite her bath she was still pretty stinky, and up close I could see how flaky her skin was. But how could I resist giving her a cuddle when she looked up at me with those big brown eyes?

Pickles fell asleep in my lap as I caught up on some paperwork. It warmed my soul to see her so relaxed with me already. She was certainly responsive to some TLC, and I vowed to give her plenty more in the weeks to come.

When it was time to go to the vet's I wrapped her up in her pink blanket and put her back in the crate she'd ridden in on the drive back from Wales. I didn't want to try her with a lead and collar just yet. For starters, she was still so unsteady on her feet, but I have also known plenty of rescues to respond with horror when you first try to clip them on a lead. If a dog hasn't got used to wearing a collar as a puppy it can come as quite a shock, and they jump around like a caught fish on a line. I certainly didn't want to panic Pickles at this point.

We drove the short distance to the surgery in the nearby town of Wendover, which was already one of my regular haunts, despite my recent arrival in the area. When you've got four dogs of your own and work with a menagerie on a daily basis, you'd better get on first-name terms with the local vet pretty quickly. Luckily, I had fallen on my feet with Michelle, the cool-headed vet at Wendover Heights surgery. She had such a calm yet loving way with the animals that I always trusted her judgement.

The clinic was bright and modern, with a half-full waiting room of excitable puppies, stately elderly dogs and crates from which the wide eyes of cats and rabbits peered. I had no sooner taken my seat on one of the Formica chairs than I was called into Michelle's consulting room, was which was plastered with various animal anatomy posters.

Michelle was waiting for us, her short, curly brown hair tucked neatly behind her ears. I'd guess she was just a few years younger than me, about thirty, and she was completely unflappable. She loved looking after my little gang of animals and would always see us at the drop of a hat, which was useful because there seemed no end to the reasons that brought me rushing over to Wendover Heights with one of my many furry charges.

'What have we got this time then, Julie?' she asked, peering into Pickles's crate.

'I think what we have is a bit of a challenge, and I'm going to need all the help I can get,' I told her. Michelle lifted Pickles out and tutted under her breath as she gently examined her, taking in her open sores and the patches where her hair was missing.

'Looks like she's been through quite an ordeal, the poor thing,' Michelle said as she watched Pickles stagger slightly on her weakened legs. 'Let me guess: she was a breeding bitch on a puppy farm?'

'That's right,' I replied. 'They reckon she could have had up to six litters – one every time she was in season.' Michelle sighed with annoyance – as a vet, she knew exactly the damage this kind of punishing breeding schedule can do.

Pickles could never have been to the vet before, but she showed no fear as Michelle peered inside her ears and mouth, although she flinched a bit as the vet touched her sore skin. In fact, she was too excited to be nervous, having a good old sniff of Michelle and spinning around trying to get a look at the whole room. I had never known a dog who had been pushed so close to death's door yet seemed to have such a thirst for life. It gave me a dash of hope; Pickles's will to live was strong.

'Your main problem is the stomach infection,' Michelle was telling me. 'Until she's eating properly it will be hard for her to fight off the other diseases. I'll give you some steroid cream and some antibacterial shampoo for her skin, some drops for her ears and some Pro-Kolin to settle her stomach.

'Keep her on a nice bland diet and make sure she eats little and often. Once her digestion is a bit more normal we can start her on some antibiotics, but they would just make her even more ill if I gave them to you now. She's going to need a lot of nursing.'

'Thanks, Michelle,' I said as I wrapped Pickles up in her blanket and put her back in the crate.

'You know me – I'm not afraid of a challenge.' I sounded more confident than I was. My head was spinning: I had known there was a lot wrong with Pickles, but it still was a shock to hear it all spelled out by Michelle. It sounded like it might take some time to get Pickles healthy – though of course I hadn't expected a quick fix.

'Puppy farms are hotbeds of disease,' Michelle said. 'It's lucky Pickles got out when she did.'

Michelle must have seen the worry on my face as she showed me to the door – surely it couldn't be too late to fix Pickles?

'She's a fighter, Julie,' Michelle said gently, putting a hand on my arm. 'She'll get there – we'll make sure of it.' I wanted desperately to believe her. I knew Pickles wouldn't give up – and I owed it to her not to give up either.

Chapter Eight

Risky Business

As I drove back to my cottage, I started to run through some calculations in my head. *What a Girl Wants* started filming fourteen weeks from now. That was a pretty normal amount of time to train up a dog for a part. Usually we would spend a couple of weeks just nurturing the dog and building the relationship, especially if the animal was a rescue. Then we would have about twelve weeks of actual training, starting with basic commands and moving on to running through the moves and tricks they would need for their specific scenes in the film.

But there was no way Pickles was going to be up to starting training in a fortnight's time. The poor mite was still so weak – too ill to even start taking the medicine that would hopefully make her better. Plus, she had so much to learn. I would have to start with toilet training and putting her on the lead before I could even think about the basics like sit and stay.

Not that the basics would be enough for the part I hoped she would play. I'd read the script, and there were some complicated moves to master. As well as a retinue of tricks, the chosen dog would also have to perform some of them in a busy crowd scene – a huge task for a dog like Pickles, considering she had barely had contact with humans before now, and many of the ones she had encountered had treated her with unimaginable cruelty. It wouldn't be enough for her to just learn the tricks – I also had to somehow erase the horrors of her past and ensure she was confident, trusting and fearless.

Despite all this, I was still sure Pickles could do it. Every situation she had been thrown into since I brought her home – even the vet's, which a lot of dogs don't like – she had taken completely in her stride. There was a boldness about her despite her diminutive size, and an open, friendly nature which seemed almost miraculous given the way she had been abused. I thought perhaps, if we could have her back to full health in a month, she might be one of those special dogs who would only need nine or ten weeks to train, and given that the Yorkie from the bank advert was experienced, if in a month or so Pickles wasn't better then at least I had a back-up plan.

When I got back to the cottage, I wasn't surprised to see Jo's Volvo parked outside. She hadn't told me she was coming but I knew she would be unable to resist meeting Pickles.

'Let's see this little soldier then!' she called as

I climbed out of the car. Jo was a couple of years younger than me, with the kind of face that always settled into a naturally cheerful expression. As usual, her fair hair was pulled back from her face in a bun and she was wearing our unofficial uniform of jeans and a cosy jumper.

'All right, all right,' I said, hoisting Pickles's crate onto my hip. 'But first – tea.' I tossed her the house keys and she unlocked the door, holding it open for me.

As Jo put the kettle on, I set the crate down in front of the Aga and coaxed Pickles out. She emerged tentatively onto the terracotta tiles, stumbling a little on her weak and spindly legs. I could tell she was exhausted from her trip to see Michelle but still managed to wag her tail when Jo crouched down to her level. A little nervous to see a new face, she backed towards me and I put a reassuring hand on the top of her head. She leaned into me, and I could see her visibly relax.

'Look how bonded she is to you already,' said Jo. 'Just amazing, that she can trust humans after what she's been through.'

'She's certainly one amazing little terrier,' I said. 'But is this too much of a crazy gamble?'

Jo smiled. 'It's not a gamble when it's a win-win,' she said. 'If we can train her for the movie – brilliant. But if we can't, you've still got one very special pet who is going to repay your kindness with all the love in the world.'

I knew she was right – it was what we always told each other every time we picked up a rescue animal, not knowing if they would be able to master the training or not. Even if they ended up not working as film dogs, we always found them a loving home with one of our network of friends and contacts – or kept them ourselves, of course.

Pickles tottered away to her bed and we watched as she curled up on her nest of blankets, giving a little sigh as she got herself comfortable. It was such a small thing to be able to give a dog somewhere warm and dry to bed down, but I felt so grateful that I was able to do this for her.

'Funny that you called her Pickles, though,' joked Jo as I topped up our tea. 'We'll certainly be in one if we're not ready in time!'

We both laughed, but it was a serious point. The production team would be in touch any day, wanting confirmation that I had found a suitable dog and expecting photos and video. In just over three months, they would expect me on set with a Yorkie who could do everything they asked, and there would be no room for excuses. Furthermore, if we couldn't deliver on this project then Birds & Animals UK might be over before it had even properly started. But whatever pressure I was under, I was determined Pickles wouldn't be rushed. She had shown extraordinary trust in me thus far and now it was my turn to put my trust in her.

Chapter Nine

Dog Days

My focus was set on trying to undo the awful damage the puppy farm had done to Pickles. Over the next few weeks, I began to nurse her slowly back to health. As I had expected, it was a slow process. Small, regular portions of chicken and rice started to settle her stomach and build up her strength. I taught her to go outside when she needed to relieve herself, and she picked it up far easier than I had anticipated. In fact, it seemed almost a relief for her to have a specified part of the garden to use as her toilet – it brought home to me how much she must have hated the dirty conditions of the puppy farm.

The other dogs had taken to Pickles like she was their sister, and it was adorable how gentle they were with our new arrival. Even boisterous Dalmatian Lala took extra care around Pickles, as if she knew how fragile she was. She and Ginelli, the red boxer, still played their rowdy games of tug of war and chase but they seemed to have a special respect for Pickles, despite her diminutive size. Ever the gentleman, white boxer George was very protective and would trail around after her, making sure she was OK. He would move off his bed – in prime position in front of the Aga – when he could tell she wanted a snooze.

Even Gypsy, my diva-like poodle, had softened towards Pickles, it was impossible not to when she was such a sweet little soul. I caught them one morning, curled up together at Gypsy's favourite end of the sofa, and I knew they would be firm friends.

While the other dogs got their usual three walks a day, one long one and a couple of short strolls, as well as a couple of fifteen-minute training sessions, Pickles had to stay behind as she still wasn't strong enough.

Instead, we practised wearing a collar and lead in the house. I thought she might struggle but she looked at me with total trust as I slipped her collar on, as if to say, *If you think it's OK, Mum, then I do too.*

For her skin problems, I was still giving her regular baths with the special shampoo I had got from the vet's. Lathering her coat took me right back to my days as a doggie hairdresser in Harrow. It felt like a distant memory now, but this had once been my daily occupation.

Ever since I was little I had dreamed of working at the dog grooming parlour, Mucky Pups, which was around the corner from my house. So at fourteen I got a Saturday job there and at sixteen I left school to work there full time, starting as a washer and working my way up to a fully qualified groomer. It was noisy and furry and busy in the salon – and I loved it. Surrounded by dogs all day, figuring out their different personalities and how to reward them with lots of fuss and treats, really was a dream come true for me.

My boss christened me the 'dog whisperer' and I always got assigned the trickiest canine customers. I found that no matter how nervous or aggressive a dog was when it first arrived, I could find a way to make them stand happily and obediently while I washed and groomed them. I quickly learned that if you could work out what made a dog tick, you could find a way to get them to trust you – a lesson that's stayed with me.

It was a job I adored, and I might still be in the grooming parlour now if a new ambition hadn't been sparked when I was nineteen. At the time, I was dating a guy whose dad was an art director for films. He was shooting a very low-budget movie which needed a dog, so he asked me if I'd be able to bring one along. I borrowed an obedient spaniel, Ben, from a client at the salon and together we shot our first movie scene, me standing just off camera and giving the dog the commands. Ben was a natural – or maybe we both were? Either way, my boyfriend's dad was delighted, and I was too.

It was my first time on a movie set and I immediately fell in love with this strange world. I loved the hustle and bustle of it all, the way the crew moved around you like a well-oiled machine, bringing a fantasy world to life in front of your very eyes. I was fascinated by the attention to detail; the cast and crew tirelessly shooting the same thing over and over, from various angles, until it was just right. It felt like I had been given a golden ticket to step behind the curtain and see how magic was made.

Best of all, I loved that I got to spend the whole day with Ben. I got such a thrill from seeing him perform, knowing that he was relying on me to guide him through it.

Flushed with happiness on the way home that

day, I still couldn't believe that people actually made a living from hanging around on sets with dogs. I decided there and then that I wanted to be a movie animal trainer.

Of course, that was easier said than done. I wrote to loads of training companies begging for an opportunity and heard back from hardly any. Eventually, I got offered work experience with a fairly ramshackle outfit, where I mainly learned how not to do it. The owner of the company meant well but he didn't really bother training the dogs – you would be sent off to a film set with a pooch that looked the part but barely knew the command for sit. I have too many memories of trying desperately to persuade a dog to perform while it was much more interested in sniffing around – and peeing on – its new surroundings, while an increasingly irate film crew looked on impatiently. Somehow I managed to muddle my way through, but I knew there had to be a better way.

I worked for another training company for a

bit, which was much better, but it wasn't long before I decided to set up on my own, which was the position I was in when I met Gary Gero and started working with him. I had a set idea about how I wanted to train animals, and that hasn't really changed. The key is positive reinforcement, and never losing your temper if they misbehave. Crucially, the welfare of the animals has to come first.

As I snuggled with the dogs on the sofa every evening, I would remind myself of that principle. It was a bit of a squash with all of us on one couch, but I adored being squeezed into a doggy cocoon, feeling their warm breath as they dozed together. I knew they were happy – and that meant it had been a good day.

Soon, the schedule for the film arrived in the post and it looked pretty full on. Pickles and I were required for at least ten days of filming, starting at the crack of dawn and with an undetermined finish time. She had even more scenes than I had expected and was going to be working with multiple actors. I felt a wave of nausea come over me when I thought about the fact Pickles had only just mastered toilet training, and was still nowhere near ready to learn any of the complicated tricks which were required for the film. But the priority had to be getting her well – everything else could wait.

Chapter Ten

A Special Bond

The good news was that Pickles was definitely making progress. Night after night I would stroke her back, feeling her body becoming ever healthier. She was stumbling less and her coat was showing gradual improvement. You wouldn't look at her now and think she was at death's door.

I always think animals can judge this sort of thing better than humans, so I was weirdly pleased to see Sky, my grey cat, trying to grab Pickles's tail one day. This was one of the many ways Sky liked to annoy her canine housemates, but until now she had held back from teasing Pickles. I knew that if she was doing it now, it meant she thought Pickles could take it. Sure enough, Pickles yapped away at Sky until she decided it was time to go and annoy Lala instead. It seemed my careful nursing was doing the trick.

Pickles slotted into our daily routine seamlessly. Every morning I would wake at seven and take the rest of the dogs for their morning run. When we got back, it was time for what I liked to call 'feeding time at the zoo'. All five dogs and two cats had their own bespoke feeding plan and it was like service at a busy restaurant getting it ready. I took extra care over what Pickles had, making sure she had a small portion of chicken and rice and gradually adding in bits of normal dog food each day to try to get her stomach used to it.

While the animals were eating, I would cook the treats for that day's training – often sausages or boiled chicken. By then Jo would have arrived, and we would run through what training we needed to complete that day, then head up with the animals to our little farm on the edge of the village, which acts as a training ground. It was a small place – a couple of clapboard barns surrounded by a handful of rolling green paddocks. When you are training multiple animals – like I was on *Harry Potter* – it helped to have a bit more space. The farm was also where I housed the animals that I couldn't take back to the cottage, like the pigs which would star in *Bridget Jones: The Edge of Reason*, for example. In that movie the pigs would have to crowd round Renée Zellweger after her character accidentally parachutes into their pen – but later they had a much more peaceful existence out on my little farm.

At lunchtime I was back at my cottage for lots of cuddles with Pickles before a quick walk with George, Ginelli, Lala and Gypsy. I wanted to spend as much time as possible with Pickles, building up our relationship, so I left the afternoon training sessions to Jo, while I sat with Pickles in my lap and ran through some paperwork. Then it was time for another walk and some grooming before a well-deserved evening snooze for us all on the sofa.

With so many animals involved the days could be a little chaotic, but there was a calmness about Pickles's unwavering devotion to me. It almost broke my heart to see how she responded to the smallest acts of kindness. As Jo had predicted, my attention to Pickles was repaid with a love that felt almost overwhelming. She would look up at me like I was her entire world. If I went into the kitchen or the bathroom she would trot after me and try to curl herself up on my foot as soon as I stood still. It was as if she needed to be in physical contact with me at all times, afraid that one day I would disappear.

'I'm not going anywhere,' I would soothe her. 'You're stuck with me now, don't you worry.'

To be honest, I was as in love with her as she

was with me. All my dogs are special to me in their own ways, and with Pickles it was that she was a comfort. I would chat away to the dogs all day – that's what happens when you live alone – but it was Pickles who really seemed to be listening. It may sound stupid but I just felt like she understood me, and I found myself pouring out all my worries about the new business venture, the times when I missed my friends back in Harrow, and anything else that was on my mind. She'd fix me with that soulful stare of hers as if to say, 'I get it.' She was my constant companion and best friend, there for me just as I was there for her.

Although she was looking better and stronger, there were moments when I was reminded how far she still had to go. She decided one day to try to climb the stairs, chasing after Sky, but the strain it put on her little legs was too much and they collapsed beneath her, sending her tumbling back down. I rushed to help her up, devastated by the bewildered look on her little face as she struggled to understand that she had been let down by her own body.

Then there was the first day I started her on a full bowl of normal dog food, believing her stomach was finally settled enough. Within hours she was as sick as she was on that very first day I brought her home. It was frustrating – even baby steps were too fast, it seemed.

Every time we faced one of these setbacks I would be thrown into a whirl of anxiety about whether I was doing the right thing, or whether I was just crazy to think a puppy-farm dog could make it in the movies. But then I would see the resilience with which Pickles faced her problems. If she fell down, she got back up again. If she got sick, she refused to let it dampen her spirits. And even if it was sometimes a case of two steps forward, one step back – well, that was still one step forward overall.

I believed in Pickles. Now that her skin and coat were looking better, I decided it was time to commit her to the project properly. One morning when the light was just right, I snapped some pictures of her in the garden and emailed them to the *What a Girl Wants* producers.

'Meet Pickles – a pup fit for a princess!' I wrote. 'Training is about to begin but I hope you'll agree she's got the look you are after.'

I clicked send before I could talk myself out of it. By the end of the day, I had a reply. The production coordinator wrote that he thought she looked perfect and they were excited to have her on board. So that was it – they were expecting Pickles, so it was time for the hard work to begin.

Chapter Eleven

Social Animal

Now that I had officially put forward Pickles for the movie, the pressure was on. Her health was still the most important thing to me, but I was aware that time was rushing by. I didn't feel Pickles was ready to start training yet, but in the meantime there were other things we could work on, like her socialisation.

As much as I would have loved to keep her all to myself, I knew if Pickles was going to have a chance at being a movie dog I needed to get her used to lots of other people. So far, she had only really got to know me, Jo and Michelle.

She had been living with me for just over a month when I decided a trip out to socialise would be good for her. If I was honest, it would be good for me too.

I was a bit of a recluse at the time. Jo would always say to me, 'You need to get out more!' And I had to admit she had a point. My life was devoted to my job – I was either cocooned with my animals working on their training, or putting in incredibly antisocial hours on film sets. The long days and travelling to locations all over the country generally meant my social life took a back seat.

Ever since I had moved to Long Marston I had been telling myself I would try out the local pubs – but somehow there was always an excuse just to stay at home with the dogs instead. Well, the time for excuses was over. Pickles needed to face the big wide world, and it was about time I did the same.

So, one Friday evening I dressed Pickles in a

sweet little tartan coat I'd bought her, and ran a comb through her unruly hair. 'Ready to paint the town red!' I joked. It suddenly occurred to me that if Pickles was making an effort, then so should I. Twenty minutes later I was dressed in blue jeans, ankle boots and a loose black top, my straight blond hair freshly washed and blow-dried. Fiddling around with my hair in the mirror, I became gradually aware of a pair of eyes on me. I looked down and saw Pickles staring up at me with a look of what I hoped was approval on her face. 'Thanks very much,' I said to her. 'You don't look too bad yourself.'

Cradling Pickles in my arms, I set off for the Queen's Head. On the short walk there I started to feel a bit nervous. Yes, Pickles was incredibly bonded to me, and was friendly and relaxed with Jo, but how would she respond to other people?

The Queen's Head is a charming, double-fronted building in the centre of the village, painted white and supposedly over five hundred years old. I ducked in through the low front door and was immediately hit by the warmth inside. The pub had tons of historical character, with wood-panelled walls, oak beams and a roaring open fire. It was also packed, filled with the laughter and chatter of locals.

I hoped that the unfamiliar environment wouldn't put Pickles on edge. But I quickly realised I shouldn't have worried. Within minutes of entering the pub and finding us a spot by the bar, I could tell Pickles was a naturally people-loving dog. In fact, she was a proper flirt. She strained at her lead in an effort to get a good sniff of the pairs of feet walking by. None of the other drinkers seemed able to resist her. They would bend down to give her lots of fuss and she just loved the attention, parting her mouth in that expression which I couldn't help thinking of as a smile.

As they stopped to pet Pickles, I found myself chatting to various villagers. By the time I had finished my first drink I realised I had met more of my neighbours in the past hour than I had during the two months I had lived in the cottage. It was clearly a very friendly community and my fears about going to the pub on my own had been unfounded. Of course, it helped to have such a cute wing-woman. Pickles was like a living, breathing conversation starter.

I had turned back to the barman to order another glass of white wine when I felt Pickles making a fuss by my feet. A tall man with mousy brown hair was squeezing past her – and, God forbid, he hadn't stopped to pet her! Pickles couldn't understand it, and seemed determined to get his attention. When he turned his back on her so he could order a pint, I heard her give an indignant little yap.

'Sorry about my dog,' I said. 'It's her first time in a pub and I think she's decided everyone's here to see her!'

The man turned towards me, and I realised with a jolt how handsome he was. He laughed.

'There are worse reasons to come to a pub, I suppose.' Taking a sip of beer, he looked down at her. Pickles gazed right back, wagging her tail expectantly.

'Oh, go on then,' he said, and crouched down to tickle her behind her ears. Pickles wiggled her whole body in delighted pleasure. 'I don't usually make a fuss of dogs because I'm allergic, but I'll make an exception for one this pretty.'

'Oh, don't let her hear you say that,' I joked back. 'It will go to her head!'

'What's her name?' he asked as he straightened back up.

'Pickles,' I replied. 'And I'm Julie.'

'I'm Glenn,' he said. 'Now, I'm pretty new around here, but you must be even newer – I've not seen you in the pub before, have I?'

'Guilty,' I said. 'I moved into the village a couple of months ago but I guess I forgot that you don't need to keep yourself to yourself like everyone does in London!'

It turned out Glenn had moved to Long Marston just a month or so before me. He sold oak furniture for a living, although he said his real dream was to one day run a pub like this one. I told him about my job too, and he was immediately fascinated. There was something about him that made me feel like I had already known him for years. We got chatting, swapping stories and making each other laugh, and before I knew it the pub was closing and we were emerging blinking into the street.

After the warmth of the pub, the evening air felt cool, and I hugged Pickles tight against me.

'I'm this way,' said Glenn, indicating the opposite direction from my cottage. 'But it's been a pleasure to make your acquaintance, Julie. And yours, Pickles,' he added, ruffling her hair a final time. 'It's not every day you get to meet a future movie star.' I giggled as he stifled a sneeze – he had been serious about that allergy.

'I'm sure we'll see you in the pub again soon,' I told him. 'It's going to be hard to keep Pickles away.'

'I'll make sure of it,' he smiled, waving as he headed off home.

As I hurried back towards the cottage through the quiet, moonlit streets, I couldn't help but smile to myself. The evening had turned out even better than I could have hoped. Pickles had done herself proud and I felt more confident than ever that she had the sort of personality to be a good film dog. 'You're a little show-off, aren't you?' I teased her. 'I can already see you fitting in with the A-listers.'

And that wasn't all either. In Glenn, with his quick sense of humour and kind eyes, I had my first village friend. Or, I wondered, as I thought back to the way our hands had brushed as we reached for the door at the end of the night, and how he had held my gaze for just a second too long, could he be more?

Chapter Twelve

Starting School

When I woke up the next morning I was shocked to find I had a slightly sore head. I don't know why I was surprised – it had been years since I had more than two glasses of wine in the evening. The headache felt more than worth it, though, and I wondered when I would see Glenn again.

Dogs have got no respect for hangovers, and they were all ready for their first walk of the day, even if I wasn't. Pickles had started joining us for a 7 A.M. stroll as she could now manage one walk a day, and it was good to stretch her legs before breakfast. I knew I would feel better once I was up and out, and sure enough, after a brisk walk across the fields, I felt the cobwebs had been blown away.

Back at the cottage I got the dogs' breakfast ready and brewed myself a strong coffee. As they gulped down their feed I opened my inbox on the laptop. My stomach turned when I saw an email from the first assistant director on *What a Girl Wants* sitting there. He was asking for an update on how training was going. My eyes flicked to the calendar on the wall – it was only about ten weeks until filming started. I would usually be two weeks into training by now.

Taking a gulp of coffee to steady my nerves, I started typed a reply:

> Hi Nick,
>   Great to hear from you! We've made a promising start, and I will get

you a full progress report by the end
of the week.
　Best wishes
　Julie

I would have to hope that would be enough to
reassure him for now – and that I would have something to say in the progress report I'd promised.

Pickles hadn't been strong enough to start
training yet, but as I watched her enthusiastic-
ally licking her bowl clean I wondered if it was
finally time. She was a different dog from the
dirty and traumatised creature I had brought
home five weeks ago. Her mange had almost
entirely cleared up; her once patchy coat was
growing back and was starting to get a lustre to
it. She was no longer unsteady on her feet; her
ears were finally free of mites; and her belly no
longer sagged as it once had. Those brown eyes,
with which she stared at me with so much love,
were bright and alert. Her performance in the

pub last night was proof of how much she had grown in confidence.

The change had happened so gradually that it almost came as a surprise to see such a healthy-looking dog in front of me. But was she really ready to train?

I got up and retrieved my bait belt from a cupboard in the kitchen. This is a sort of pouch I wear while training, with a pocket full of tasty treats to encourage the dogs to learn new things. As soon as I put it on, the other dogs started bouncing around in excitement. They had all been trained with one of these, and I still kept up regular training with them all, even though they weren't filming for anything, because I knew how much they enjoyed it. For them, the bait belt could mean only one thing – there were treats on offer.

I ran through a few moves with the bigger dogs one at a time in the garden (excusing Lala, who didn't like training – we played fetch instead), so they weren't disappointed. I had been teaching

George how to nudge an object along the floor, so we practised that with an empty Tupperware pot. He had to push it along with his nose on my instruction, and he was getting really good at it. The Tupperware was nice and light – we would make it trickier with something bulkier and heavier next time. Gypsy and Ginelli happily ran through their back catalogue of roll over, beg, walk backwards and heel, getting a treat every time they got it right.

Once the bigger dogs had had their fair share of attention, I took them back into the kitchen and brought Pickles out into the garden. 'Sorry, guys,' I told them. 'The new pupil needs to concentrate.' Pickles looked up at me expectantly. Now was the moment of truth. How would she respond to this?

As always, I decided to start off nice and easy. I walked a few paces away and crouched down to her level, and called her to come towards me. 'Come, come, come, Pickles!' I called, and she danced eagerly into my arms. That wasn't too much of a challenge – she already responded to her name and she never wanted to be very far from me anyway. 'Good girl!' I told her. She got a treat every time she came correctly, and I could see her warming to the task – this was fun.

Next, I showed her a treat in my hand and told her, 'Sit.' This is how I tend to work: give the dog a command, show them a reward, and let them try to figure out what they need to do to get it. Some dogs can take ages to make the connection between the command and how they need to respond. Others get it with just a few training sessions.

Pickles looked at me quizzically, wondering what she needed to do. She tried coming closer – 'Uh-uh!' I said, to show her this wasn't what I wanted right now. She stopped, then sat right down. 'Sit!' I said straight away, and gave her the treat and lots of 'good girls'. She wriggled happily. That was astonishingly fast – usually dogs will try all sorts before they give up and sit down. But was it just a fluke?

'That was very impressive, Pickles,' I said. 'But let's see if you can do it again.'

I got another treat out. 'Sit,' I said. She plonked her bottom down straight away. I could hardly believe it. 'Well done, Pickles!' I exclaimed, bending down to give her plenty of fuss as she skipped excitedly in a circle.

We tried it several more times and Pickles got it right again and again. She would sit before I even had the full command out of my mouth, then jump up excitedly for the treat. It can take hours to teach a dog their first command, but here she was nailing it straight out of the blocks.

Best of all, I could tell she was sincerely enjoying it. Her trademark 'smile' was plastered all over her face and she was wagging her tail so much that her whole body vibrated. She looked like she could have done it all day long, but I like to keep training sessions short when a dog is starting off, so after fifteen minutes we drew to a close.

'Don't worry, Pickles,' I told her as I unclipped my bait belt, 'we can do some more later.'

I was trying hard not to let myself get carried away, but I was seriously excited by what I had just seen. Had I inadvertently stumbled across a superstar?

Chapter Thirteen

Practice Makes Perfect

While it had been immensely satisfying to nurse Pickles back to health, it felt really good to get down to training. It's what I had always loved to do, and in a weird way I think I was destined to make a career out of it. I still get a buzz out of building up that communication between human and animal, a feeling I had first encountered in childhood.

Over the years I've trained all sorts of animals: not just dogs and cats but pigs, goats, reindeer, rabbits, rats, ravens, owls – even snakes. But it's training dogs that always takes me back to where it all began.

When I was growing up, long before I knew that the job of 'movie animal trainer' existed, I had been obsessed with teaching tricks to my dog, Sally, a rescued Border collie cross.

My parents had finally given in to years of begging and got Sally for me when I was eleven. I came home from school on my birthday and this gorgeous black and white bundle of fur came running out of the utility room. I cried for days out of sheer joy and had to keep getting up in the night to check Sally was real.

From that moment on, Sally was my best friend. I would spend hours and hours in the garden 'training' her, even though I really didn't have a clue what I was doing. It didn't seem to matter that I didn't have a manual, though; I got to know how Sally's mind worked and she in turn seemed to learn what I was trying to say. Nothing beat the feeling of her nailing roll over or high five. We were a little team.

I was pleased to say I had honed my technique somewhat since those days, but I still saw training as an exercise in tuning a human mind into that of an animal. In my experience, it was important to keep training sessions short but frequent, which is why I would let Pickles have a play or a rest before trying again.

My usual approach is to spend the first couple of weeks of training doing six fifteen-minute sessions each day, during which I teach the basics like sit, stay and lie down. When the dog is ready to move on to more complicated tricks like standing on their hind legs (so long as their size and weight can take it), moving backwards, crawling on their belly or barking on command, we move to longer sessions of thirty minutes, about four times a day.

That might not sound like much, but I'm usually working with several animals at any one time so, along with keeping on top of the day-to-day running of the business and the grooming, exercise and general care of my animals, as well as casting for our upcoming projects, that is enough to keep me very busy. I also have to keep track of how many treats each animal has had during training, so I can adjust their meals accordingly and make sure they are eating a healthy, balanced diet. The most important thing, however, is to only train an animal for as long as he or she is engaged and enjoying it – the worst thing you can do is make training something they dread. If it becomes a battle between you and the animal, it's all over.

With the first day's filming of *What a Girl Wants* looming ever closer, I didn't have the time to spend weeks and weeks with Pickles going over the basic moves. But I sensed that she might not need it anyway.

By the time I clipped the bait belt on that afternoon, she knew what to expect. The morning's session had been no one-off, and she had perfected come and sit by the end of the day.

Over the next few days we got stuck in, moving on to lie down, turn around, and stand on a mark. She perfected them all. It was mind-blowing – what that dog learned in a week would usually take me a month to teach.

Pickles was such a clever little dog, but what really clinched it was her devotion to me. Just one look at her trusting face and I knew she would try to do anything to please me. For her, training wasn't just about the treats – it was about the praise, and knowing she had made me happy. Working with her was a joy.

A couple of days in, Jo popped round to see how we were getting on. Sometimes the presence of another person can throw a dog completely; they're so distracted by this new face that everything they have learned goes out the window. Of course, this was not the case with Pickles. Her eyes never left my face as we ran through come, sit and lie down.

'Now that's a partnership!' cried Jo, applauding as we reached the end of our fifteen-minute session. 'I can't believe what you've taught her in such a short space of time!'

I was crouched on the floor with Pickles, burying my face in her tawny fur as she happily licked my face. I had been wondering if I had simply got too attached to this little dog and convinced myself I had made more ground with her than I really had, but from Jo's reaction I could see that wasn't the case.

'I was starting to think I was hallucinating how good she was,' I said to Jo. 'I'm glad you're here to prove I'm not going mad.'

'Definitely not mad,' said Jo. 'You know I sometimes think your plans are crazy, but somehow it pays off.'

I felt a burst of gratitude that I had spent so much time and effort on getting Pickles well. Those precious weeks had created a dog who was utterly besotted with me, to the point that I suspected I might not even need the treats during our training sessions.

Her progress was so miraculously rapid that I decided not to wait until the end of the week to email the director. I wrote him a list of everything Pickles had learned so far, marvelling to myself at how quickly she had picked everything up, and attached a few short videos showing how she was getting on.

'Don't worry about a thing,' I wrote. 'This dog is going to be a star.'

Chapter Fourteen

Working Like a Dog

Now that I had reassured the movie bosses that Pickles was going to be great it was time to step up her training so that I could deliver on my promise, because over the next few days I started to regret my rash email. Was I really certain that there was nothing to worry about? Pickles's health issues seemed to be under control but they could rear their head again at any time. She had picked up the basics fast, but would she continue to make such rapid progress as we moved on to more complicated things? And even if she could perform in the familiar environment of my garden, could she replicate it on a hectic film set?

I knew that the only way to quell my anxiety was to take every day as it came, and to continue to put my trust in Pickles. Luckily she made what could have been an uphill struggle seem easy.

Over the next few weeks Pickles went from strength to strength. She loved our training sessions so much that they seemed to be healing her from the inside out. Fitter than ever, she was now up to joining the rest of the dogs for their evening exercise as well as the morning walk. And when I groomed her, I saw that her coat was starting to get a gorgeous auburn glow. It was almost as if all the years of trauma and pain were dropping away with every new trick she learned, until she was practically a puppy again.

I still couldn't believe how quickly she was picking everything up. She just loved the challenge and was so eager to please. I started teaching her things she didn't need to learn just because I could, in case they came in useful. That's how she learned how to jump through a hoop and walk on her hind legs – not that there was much call for either in the script!

Although she had picked up sit quickly, we had to build up the time she would remain in that position. When you teach your dog to sit at home they will usually do it for about twenty seconds, but on a film set that is nowhere near long enough. Teaching a dog to stay in position can be harder to teach than the position itself because they get excited and distracted. Pickles's active little mind always wanted to move on to the next thing, so it took plenty of patience to teach her to be, well, patient.

The thing I spent the most time on was teaching Pickles to go to a mark. This is crucial as it allows us to position the dog exactly where the director wants them for the shot. The mark is basically a small wooden block, and I teach the dog to go and put their front paws on it, wherever it happens to be. Then you make it more complicated by adding multiple marks and teaching the dog to go between them on command.

Another thing Pickles had to learn was how to look at someone other than me when she was doing her scenes. A dog working with a trainer – especially one as bonded to their handler as Pickles was to me – will keep their eyes on you at all times, which can look a bit unnatural when their owner is meant to be the actor they are sharing a scene with.

I had enlisted Jo's help so I could teach Pickles to engage with someone else while still listening for commands from me. 'Look at her, look at her,' I told Pickles as she sat in Jo's arms. Jo had to remain quiet, because Pickles still had to know her commands were coming from me. It was obviously a bit unnatural for Pickles at first, but like everything else she picked it up in no time.

'I thought you couldn't teach an old dog new

tricks?' said Glenn over dinner in the pub one evening. We had started meeting regularly – first by accident, then on purpose. Sometimes we would meet in the pub, other times he would join me for long dog walks as we explored the countryside we were both getting used to calling home. Officially, we were just friends, although I didn't have any other friends who gave me butterflies in my stomach when they walked in the door.

I smiled, reaching over to pinch one of his chips. 'Just another myth that Pickles has proved wrong!' I explained that, in my experience, the age of the dog doesn't really matter. What does matter is how interested they are in food, toys or praise – as long as you have a dog which is really motivated by one of those things, you can definitely train them.

'Sounds like most men,' grinned Glenn. If only it was that easy, I thought to myself. Dogs I understood – men were far more complicated. Glenn was a case in point: did he like me like I liked him, or was he just being friendly? I tried to put the thought out of my mind.

'Listen, I need your help with something,' I told him as he poured me another glass of red wine.

'Anything for you, Jules,' he said. 'What is it?'

'Well, Pickles has a big scene where she has to run through a crowd,' I replied. 'She's going to need to practise being around a large amount of people she doesn't know. So—'

'So you thought Mr Popular here could source you a crowd,' finished Glenn. 'Not a problem. Shall we say Saturday morning behind the village hall?'

'Er, OK,' I said. It was Thursday evening. 'That's very soon . . .'

Glenn winked. 'I've got the contacts, don't you worry. The crowd of your dreams will be assembled.'

I knew Glenn wouldn't let me down, but I felt suddenly nervous. In just two days' time Pickles would be performing in public for the first time. My training was about to be put to the test.

Chapter Fifteen

Crowd Control

When I woke on Saturday morning, I was dismayed to hear the rain pattering on my window. After weeks of glorious sunshine it was a dismal, drizzly day. It didn't bode well for getting a crowd of volunteers to stand around outside.

Like the princess that she clearly believed she was, Pickles had long since taken to sleeping on the end of my bed, curled in a furry ball in the folds of my stripy duvet cover. As soon as I stirred, she was up like a spring, excited for whatever new experience I planned to throw at her that day. 'Time to expand your social circle,' I told her this morning as I rummaged in my wardrobe for a clean pair of jeans.

Pickles was such a friendly little thing that I wasn't concerned that the crowd would spook her, but I did expect her to get distracted. Like that first time I had taken her to the pub, she seemed to believe that other people existed purely to pet her, and she was going to make damn certain she got the attention she deserved.

In the film, there was a scene set at the Queen's garden party, and Pickles would have to run through the assembled guests to find Amanda Bynes. She had learned the moves, but now it was time to see if she could pull them off amid the excitement of a crowd of new people.

After Pickles had played a manic game of chase with Lala in the garden, observed lazily by

George, I decided she must have got some of her morning giddiness out of her system. It was 10 A.M. by the time all the dogs had been fed and exercised, and then I headed to the village hall, Pickles prancing along in front of me on her red lead. The hall was a flat-roofed, square building in the middle of the village, and was where Glenn had instructed me to meet him and his 'crowd'. I was hoping for maybe a dozen people, which wasn't exactly garden-party sized but would be a good start. Any practice Pickles could get would be valuable.

But as I approached I heard a growing hubbub of voices, which sounded like a lot more than twelve people. I ducked behind the hall and was astonished to see a throng of nearly a hundred assembled on the recreation ground, including dozens of children tearing around. Some faces I recognised, but there were many I had never seen before. Grinning, Glenn greeted me with a hug. 'Will this do?'

'Just about!' I said, amazed. 'Who on earth are all these people?'

'There's most of the lads from the rugby team and their families,' said Glenn, pointing to a group of towering blokes who couldn't have been anything else. 'There's Mick and Gemma who run the pub. I asked them to round up as many of their regulars as they could, and they came up trumps. There's a couple of the guys I work with, and the rest are all your neighbours – once I started asking around everyone was pretty excited to be involved in training cinema's next big thing.'

'You're just amazing,' I said, then stopped myself, feeling the colour rise in my cheeks. 'I mean – this is amazing. Thank you.'

Glenn smiled. 'Like I said: anything for you.'

The moment was promptly broken by Pickles, who was leaping up to paw Glenn's shins. He bent down and picked her up, ruffling her hair as he always did.

'Listen up, people!' he called, and the noisy

chatter reduced to a low murmur. 'This is Pickles – and Julie, her human. Julie will tell you what she needs you to do.'

I was suddenly nervous as I felt everyone's eyes on me. 'Thank you all so much for coming!' I called, as loudly as I could. 'It means such a lot. I don't really need you to do much except just stand around and chat. I'm going to run Pickles through some of her commands and hopefully she won't get too distracted. If she does, please ignore her – I know it's easier said than done!'

There was a smattering of laughter before people turned back to their conversations. I looked down at my little dog, who was quivering with eagerness to get going. 'Right, Pickles,' I said. 'Imagine it's still just you and me. I need you to focus, OK?'

Glenn had agreed to stand in for Amanda Bynes – 'The part I was born to play,' he joked – and the idea was Pickles would run from me, through the crowd, to a mark by him.

I could sense, however, that it was all too exciting for her. She was straining at her lead already. I fished in my bait belt for a tasty bit of ham to hold her attention as I unclipped the lead.

'OK, Pickles,' I said. 'Heel.' I would start by walking through the crowd with her to the mark. Then, once she knew where it was, I would get her to run there on her own. But we had barely taken one step before she dived away from me, desperate to say hello to Harold and Geoff, who she recognised from the pub.

'Pickles!' I said sharply, and she spun back to me – only to be distracted by a couple of kids playing tag and deciding she was going to join in. 'Come back here!' I called as she tore after a little boy, who was in turn running after his sister, giggling wildly.

Everyone seemed most amused by this little dog who seemed far more intent on socialising than doing her work. I gave her the familiar commands, but instead of doing what she was told she would bounce over to someone she hadn't greeted yet, or just run in mad circles of giddy excitement. She had that open-mouthed smile on her face and couldn't get enough of all the new sounds and smells. 'I suppose I should be grateful she's not the nervous type,' I said to Glenn as she darted towards another family.

It was the first time that training with Pickles had been this chaotic, and it was a horrible feeling. This was nothing compared to what a film set would be like, with even more people, lots of strange equipment and all sorts of unfamiliar noises. How embarrassing would it be if I turned up with Pickles, promising she was perfectly trained, only to have her run riot while steadfastly ignoring me? It was absolutely crucial that she got over her giddiness and learned to focus even when there were lots of distractions.

Convinced that my neighbours must think me a complete amateur, all I wanted to do was pick up Pickles and go home. But this could be my only opportunity to train with a crowd this big, and I knew Pickles would get it, so long as I remained patient. Once I had caught up with her and calmed her down, we started from the top again. This time, I could see in her eyes she had decided to knuckle down. I could sense a change as her attention snapped back to me.

Locking eyes with her, I gave the command to run to the mark. As if it was the easiest thing in the world, she galloped straight there, without a single glance at anyone else.

'There, I knew you could do it!' I told her, giving her a big handful of ham and plenty of fuss. 'Let's try again.'

That was it: she aced it, every time. 'I think you were just testing me at the beginning, weren't you?' I said to her. I realised she just needed to get the excitement out of her system – having been deprived of human company for so long, she couldn't help herself when surrounded with so many potential playmates.

After she had done the scene perfectly enough times, I started telling people they were free to go. But most seemed reluctant to leave and Glenn, Pickles and I ended up staying for at least another hour, just chatting to people as if I were the Queen and this was my garden party. My neighbours were all keen to stress how much they wanted to help with anything else I needed, and I went away with several invitations to Sunday lunch.

As we finally headed home – bidding farewell to Glenn, who was heading to the pub with the rugby lads – I reflected on the fact that Pickles had once again found me some new friends.

'You're a little social butterfly, aren't you?' I said to her fondly, hugging her close to my chest. All those years of suffering on the puppy farm, and yet she was so outgoing and affectionate.

I think we can all be guilty of being nervous of new experiences and stepping beyond our comfort zones. Certainly, I had been for the last six months. But here was Pickles, who put all of that into perspective and showed how much could be gained from putting yourself out there. I thought I was the one teaching her, but I could now see that I was learning a lot from her too.

Chapter Sixteen

Fight or Fright

The first day of filming was drawing ever closer, but I couldn't remember a time that I had been more confident about my charge than I was with Pickles. With a shiver I remembered how I had felt on the run up to *Harry Potter*, with those owls who were anything but wise. Luckily, we got there in the end – but I certainly wouldn't be rushing to work with owls again.

My experience with Pickles couldn't be more different. With two weeks to go, we were already running though her scenes on a regular basis and I knew she had them in the bag. Of course, you never know how a dog will respond on an actual film set, but I felt happy that she was as well prepared as she could be. She was confident, obedient and full of energy – a true miracle given the state I had found her in.

The owner of the Yorkie from the bank advert, which we had been keeping on as back-up, called to say that he had been offered another job, which clashed with the filming schedule for *What a Girl Wants*, and could he take it or did we still need him? Jo and I were unanimous. Pickles was ready, and she was going to be a star – no back-up required.

'I almost feel like it's been too easy,' I said to Jo one morning as we ran through the scenes with Pickles together. 'How did we get so lucky with this little dog?'

'It's not luck!' said Jo, tickling Pickles behind her ears, making the little dog squirm with joy.

'It's down to your hard work – and hers, too. That dog is a fighter and you saw it in her from the start.'

I didn't want to get complacent, but it did feel like everything was falling into place. Pickles was perfect, Birds & Animals UK had several more jobs lined up and I felt more settled than ever in Long Marston now I had built relationships with so many of my neighbours, thanks to Pickles – and Glenn, of course. And then there was my relation-ship with him, if you could call it that.

I'd come to rely on Glenn, who could always make me laugh no matter what the occasion. Ever since we had first met there had been a spark between us, and whenever we got together for drinks in the pub or weekend walks we just couldn't stop talking. I couldn't deny that I was attracted to him – but I just wasn't sure he felt the same way. Aside from the odd glance held too long, everything was firmly in the friend zone. I was nervous to tell him how I felt, but maybe it was time to be brave? Pickles had shown me that courage paid off, after all.

I was still mulling this over when, ten days until filming started, I took Pickles and the other four dogs for our usual stroll through the woods behind my cottage. A pretty jumble of pine and oak trees, the shady woods always offered a moment of peace, however hectic the day had been. My relaxed evening walk was always one of the highlights of my day.

It was summer by now and the evening sun bathed us all in a golden glow, while bees hummed lazily amid the long grass. I gratefully breathed in the scent of fresh pine as I picked my way down the winding paths that ran through the woods, trying to spot the wood pigeons I could hear cooing gently in the trees. The dogs crashed through the undergrowth, chasing after the exciting scents of rabbits and squirrels. I loved to see how Pickles had become part of the pack with George, Ginelli, Gypsy and Lala – although on her little legs she struggled to keep up with their breakneck speeds.

While they raced ahead, Pickles trotted back to me, keeping close by like a shadow, as she always did. At every fork in the path, she would look back at me as if to say: *I'll follow you, whatever you choose.* Until just a few months ago she had never been on a walk in her life, yet here she was, as loyal and obedient as it was possible to be. For her, freedom didn't mean the chance to run far away; it meant freedom from cruelty, in exchange for companionship and security. Her strength of character would never cease to amaze me.

We reached the end of the woods, where the path opened up into a beautiful meadow, filled at this time of the year with wildflowers and cow parsley. It was here that I noticed another walker up ahead, his distant figure casting a long shadow. I couldn't see a dog, but the lead slung over his shoulder suggested he did have one somewhere.

Squinting against the low sun, I tried to make

out the man's face. Slightly built and young-looking, he was half turned away from me, but even from this angle I was pretty sure I hadn't seen him before, which was strange. After nearly six months in the village I had got to know most of the other dog-walkers. There was something about the way he was standing, too, which put me on edge. And I didn't like it that I had no idea where his dog was. Maybe he wasn't a dog-walker at all?

Hoping I was being overcautious, I whistled to my dogs and clipped a lead onto Pickles, the littlest one, just in case the mystery mutt was big and boisterous. I could hear a distant rustling and I scanned the field, trying to work out where it was coming from. I felt suddenly exposed, alarmed by the way the youth had made no effort to call his dog even though he must have noticed us enter the meadow.

Then, out of nowhere, a sudden crash. Before I even had a chance to register what was happening, an enormous dog burst from the hedgerow. Within seconds it was on us, monstrous teeth bared and a furious growl rising like thunder in its throat.

'Pickles!' I cried, seeing my little dog freeze immediately in panic. The other dog was a huge, muscly great thing and for some reason it was primed to attack. Dogs don't usually become aggressive unless they think you are on their territory or are made to feel protective over their human. Whatever had triggered it, this one was clearly after a fight.

The dog locked its eyes on Pickles, as if spotting easy prey. She dropped to the floor in instant submission and I threw myself in front of her, trying to block this terrifying aggressor. But the dog just dodged around my legs and ferociously launched itself at Pickles's neck. 'No!' I yelled. 'Get off, get off!'

The dog was snapping and snarling, and had Pickles pinned by the neck. I tried desperately to reach beneath it to grab Pickles. I couldn't reach her, so I tried to haul the dog off instead – but it twisted out of my hands. Pickles was whimpering in sheer terror and I was shouting at the dog, feeling the panic rise in my throat. My precious baby was in mortal danger and, try as I might, I couldn't get to her. I would have let the dog bite my arm off if I had to, if only I could keep her safe.

Then suddenly the mystery dog-walker was at my side, wrenching his dog away. I snatched Pickles up into my arms and frantically checked her for signs of harm. She was shaking like a leaf, but as far as I could tell, the dog hadn't managed to draw blood. Pickles was far from OK – but at least her life was no longer in immediate danger.

I turned furiously to the dog owner, who I now saw was a young lad of about twenty, with a thin pale face and an unrepentant expression. I had been right – this was someone I definitely hadn't seen before, and with his grubby tracksuit and gold chains looped round his neck he didn't look like your average village dog-walker either. He had managed to get the dog on to a lead and was trying to drag it away, but it was still straining and baring its teeth at my other four dogs, who circled timidly behind me.

'How could you be so irresponsible?' I raged, feeling my cheeks becoming hot with anger. 'Your dog could have killed mine! You shouldn't have it off the lead if it can't be trusted.'

He smirked and said nothing, just yanked the dog roughly behind him as he hurried back towards the woods, pulling a hood up to hide his face. He clearly thought I was just a hysterical woman and Pickles some stupid lapdog who did not merit his concern.

I could feel my blood boiling and I had to resist the urge to run after him and give him a proper piece of my mind. In my opinion, there is no such thing as a bad dog, only bad owners. So when you get an animal behaving as aggressively as this, without warning, you have to wonder what happened to make them act in that way. And of course, it was totally unacceptable to have such a dangerous beast off the lead and free to attack other people, dogs – even children.

But there was no point getting into a fight – I had more important things to worry about. I looked down at Pickles, bundled against my chest, who was still trembling with fear. I could see her retreating into herself, the self-confidence of moments earlier nowhere to be seen. My heart was still galloping with adrenalin but now I felt an icy rush of fear come over me. It was as if, before my very eyes, Pickles was reverting to the beleaguered, damaged dog of the puppy farm.

I couldn't believe that within a moment all our months of hard work could potentially be undone. One question was running over and over in my head: *how could this happen now?*

Chapter Seventeen

A Living Nightmare

'It's OK, little one, you're safe now,' I cooed, rocking Pickles in my arms as if she was a new-born baby. 'Let's get you home – it's all right.'

I knew it was vital that Pickles didn't see my fear and panic, but it was all I could do to keep the tremble out of my voice. She may not have been harmed physically but I had a sinking feeling that the attack had inflicted some serious mental scars.

I clipped the other dogs back onto their leads

and hurried home, taking the shortcut which ran in the opposite direction from where the youth and the dog had gone. I felt so foolish – how could it be that, just moments before, I was revelling in how easy everything had been? It was as if I had set myself up for a fall – and what a fall it had been.

I could feel the tears welling up before I was even through the cottage door. Tears for the unfairness of it all; of all dogs, Pickles did not deserve this. And tears of frustration, after all the hard work Jo and I had put in. The film started in just ten days and there was now a good chance that Pickles would be right back at square one, when half an hour ago she was in prime position.

Michelle had given me her home number to use in case of an out-of-hours emergency, and this felt like it was one. I rang her and could feel my voice shaking as I told her the whole story.

'It hasn't drawn blood, but should I bring her in to be examined anyway?' I asked.

'Probably for the best,' said Michelle. 'I can meet you at the surgery in an hour.'

Michelle was extremely fond of Pickles, having helped me nurse her back to health. We had spoken just the other day about how pleased we both were to see her flourishing. Michelle's face was pale as she gently examined Pickles now. I held my breath, hoping there was no serious damage done.

'The good news is it doesn't seem like she's been hurt,' said Michelle. 'But she's not herself, is she? She's pretty traumatised right now, but we have to hope that won't turn into long-term anxiety. I imagine she probably just needs rest and plenty of TLC, which I know you'll give her.'

Thanking Michelle, I loaded Pickles into the car and drove her home. When we got back, I carried Pickles to the sofa, where we normally sat, but she jumped straight down and hurried to her basket, where she curled herself up in a protective ball. I really started crying then. She looked so subdued, so broken; I hadn't seen her like this since the day I first met her at the rescue centre in Wales.

The other dogs could sense that something wasn't right. Gypsy, always so sweet and affectionate, came and put her head in my lap, her tail wagging sympathetically. Lala, who usually just wanted to play, was unusually calm as she jumped up on the sofa beside me and licked my hand. And the two boxers settled themselves by Pickles's bed, like a sheltering wall, which she accepted without question.

You can always rely on dogs to know just when you need them most. They have an innate emotional intelligence which goes beyond all reason. I know that to people who are not animal lovers it sounds like madness, but I really think at times they can read your mind. In that moment I felt so grateful for my little wolf pack. 'What are we going to do about your poor sister?' I asked Gypsy, stroking her curly head. 'You're probably a bit too big to be a stand-in, aren't you?'

Pickles didn't want to sleep on my bed that night, preferring to stay curled in her basket. Without the familiar sound of her breathing at my feet I couldn't sleep. The moment the dog leapt from the hedge played over and over in my mind. Could I have acted faster to pick up Pickles? Should I have noticed the dog lurking before it attacked? I knew deep down there was no point blaming myself – there was nothing more I could have done – but that didn't stop the questions tormenting me in the dark of the night. Eventually, I fell into an uneasy slumber, with dreams full of leaping shadows and the distant whimpering of a dog in pain.

The next morning, I woke with a start, and all my anxieties of the night before came flooding back in a rush as soon as I saw the empty spot at the end of the bed where Pickles would usually be. Was I going to get my happy, confident little girl back?

Wrapping myself in my dressing gown, I hurried downstairs, hoping against hope that Pickles would be back to her old self. I could tell immediately that she was not. Where usually she would be bouncing around in excitement when she could tell I was awake, today she stayed curled in a protective ball, her head bowed.

Carefully I approached her, reaching out my hand slowly in case a sudden movement startled her. When I tickled her ears she gently licked my wrist, as if to tell me we were still friends. I lifted her up and buried my head in her neck. 'I'm so sorry this has happened, Pickles,' I told her. 'But it was a one-off. You've got to trust me, OK?' I felt her tense body relax a little as I held her, allowing me to hope that her confidence in me remained.

I thought of how training had sped up her recovery before, and wondered if just getting straight back into it might help her now. Maybe a normal day's work was all she needed? It had to be worth a try.

Chapter Eighteen

Facing the Fear

After breakfast I loaded Pickles into the car and headed for my training ground on the edge of the village. Until yesterday, this had been one of Pickles's favourite places. She knew that if we were on the farm we were going to be doing plenty of training, which for her was basically playtime. As we arrived, I saw her prick her ears in anticipation, and I allowed myself to believe that everything would be all right.

I clipped on my bait belt and lead Pickles to

the paddock we always used, then started to run through her first scene. But she just couldn't concentrate. Even the smallest of noises – like the donkey kicking over his bucket in the next field, or a car door slamming in the distance – threw her off. Any sudden movement made her freeze with panic. She was jumpy and nervous, and while she still responded to most of the commands, her sparkle was gone.

After fifteen minutes I decided to stop, even though Pickles had been regularly acing half-hour sessions in the past fortnight. I could tell something would have to be done if I wanted to get her confidence back up. It was the fear of the unknown that was spooking her – she had been pretty fearless, but now she was scared of her own shadow.

We headed back to the cottage and I rang Jo. She was furious when I told her what had happened. 'So what did this man look like again?' she asked, and I could hear her fumbling with a pen and paper. 'And which direction was he heading towards? We need to find him and make sure he knows exactly what he's done. Can you report something like this to the police?'

'That was my first thought too, Jo,' I said. 'But we don't have time for all that. We have to focus on Pickles now. How are we going to get her back to her old self?'

Jo paused. 'Do you remember that black cat I had last year, Millie?' she said. 'It was a similar situation, if you remember. She got spooked on set because a man in high-vis started drilling behind her without warning. After that she was terrified of anyone in high-vis – not very useful on set.

'I had get her used to the idea that not everyone in high-vis was scary. So we had loads of people put on a high-vis then approach her and give her a treat. It was all about replacing the negative with a positive. And it worked. She was a cat, too – not a super-smart dog like Pickles.'

It was our standard approach to getting an

animal over their fear: creating a situation we could control, which would prove to them they had no reason to be afraid. In this case, that would mean taking Pickles back to the meadow and showing her that she was still safe.

Jo and I hatched a plan, to start that very evening. I would take Pickles for her usual walk, and Jo would wait for us close to the spot where the she had been attacked. She would bring a friendly dog who would hopefully prove to Pickles that what had happened on Wednesday was the exception, not the rule.

It seemed like a solid approach, but as I clipped Pickles onto her lead that evening I started to worry that it wouldn't work. As we headed towards the woods she hung back, and jumped at the slightest sound. 'It's OK, Pickles,' I soothed her. 'You're safe with me, I promise.'

I was willing her to find that courage inside her which had ensured she was a survivor, not a victim, of the puppy farm. It felt like it was vital we completed this walk – if we didn't, it would be the first time Pickles had given up on anything.

But as we approached the scene of the attack I could feel Pickles's fear pulsating through her. She pulled back on her lead with remarkable strength for such a little dog. I tried to keep calm, talking to her constantly and staying close to her side. I had a pocketful of dog treats, which I handed to her at regular intervals. She crunched them up with her usual enthusiasm, nudging my hand for another one. 'At least it hasn't affected your appetite,' I laughed, relieved that she was still open to a bribe.

Jo's familiar profile came into view, with her little Westie, Pepper, on a lead by her side. Despite Pepper's diminutive size, Pickles started to panic, digging her heels in and pulling back on the lead as she scrambled to hide behind my legs.

Hating to see her convulsed with fear, I wondered if I should pick Pickles up. But I had to trust my instinct, and something told me that our plan was going to work.

Jo loosened Pepper's lead a little and he ambled over towards Pickles, having a good old sniff. Pickles's body seemed gradually to relax as she realised Pepper was no threat, and soon her curiosity got the better of her. Peering out from behind my ankles, she sniffed him back and I could see a flash of the old, friendly Pickles.

'See, that wasn't so bad,' I told her, giving her another treat. I felt a rush of pride for my little fighter, whose open nature had always been her greatest strength.

'She already looks more confident,' said Jo. 'But let's not get ahead of ourselves. I'll meet you here the same time tomorrow.'

True to her word, the next night there was Jo again, this time with her Labrador, Raijin. Pepper was one thing, but how would Pickles cope with a much bigger dog? Once again, Pickles stiffened at the sight him, her fear palpable. Her ears twitched and she stepped backwards, and I could sense her deciding whether to bolt.

'You can do it, Pickles,' I coaxed, determined to break through her hesitancy. 'I know you're nervous, but you have to be brave. No one's going to hurt you.'

She looked up at me with those soulful eyes, taking it all in. It really was as if she understood what I was saying. I swear I could see her make the decision to trust me, before she ploughed forwards towards Raijin, a little shyer than normal but determined not to turn on her heel.

Our plan was working: by carefully introducing her to different dogs, we were getting Pickles used to dealing with unfamiliar animals again. But I was still very aware that time was running out and I had to make sure the habit was ingrained.

With this in mind, I roped in some of my neighbours and arranged for them to meet us with their dogs on different routes through the village on different evenings. The idea was to prove to Pickles that she had nothing to fear from meeting a strange dog, and that she had nothing to fear from the unknown either.

Pickles seemed to take courage from the encounters, which was exactly what we had hoped. During training sessions she was much more focused, with distant noises bothering her less. I had to hope the attack really hadn't blown us completely off course – but only time would tell.

Chapter Nineteen

The Final Countdown

I didn't have too long to stew on the possibilities of something else going wrong, because before I knew it the week before filming had arrived.

By now we were simply running through Pickles's scenes over and over again to make sure she knew them by heart, and I was reassured to see she was right back in the swing of things.

Then one morning, with just three days to go before filming, we were in the paddock on the farm when something caught my eye. It was a figure I recognised – with an all too familiar dog – cutting through the public footpath that ran along the bottom of the next field.

Pickles had noticed too. She must have been able to smell her former adversary in the air. Standing stock-still, she stared as the dog made its progress along the path.

It felt like time was suspended as we watched the dog in the distance. I could see Pickles figuring out whether to bolt or not. My heart was galloping in my chest as I waited to see what she would do, willing her not to panic. Was I about to lose her again?

Then, all of a sudden, the moment passed. Pickles turned back to me and calmly sat up on her haunches to beg – the trick we had just been practising. I laughed and bent down to give her a treat and lots of praise. 'You are such a brave girl,' I told her. 'I am so proud of you!'

Pickles still trusted me: of that much I was sure. Even though I had inadvertently led her into a dangerous situation – one I could not possibly have foreseen – I knew she would still follow me wherever I asked her to go. There was no going back to square one for this little dog, because she was so determined to leave her past behind.

I turned back to watch the man and the dog as they retreated into the distance, and realised with a jolt that the dog was on a lead. Maybe my angry words had made a difference after all, which was good news for any other dog-walkers they encountered.

Pickles and I carried on with our training session, and I was delighted to see her perfect trick after trick as she had been doing before the attack. But there was still no telling what sort of sights, smells and sounds on the film set might throw her off course. It was less than two weeks since she had been traumatised, and any progress since then felt fragile at best. But I knew I had to trust her.

On the day before filming, we went through the

scene she was scheduled to shoot the next day, and she nailed every beat. It's what I always do on the eve of a film, before taking the dog back to the cottage for a thorough bath. Movie people don't like an animal that smells a bit funny or looks too scruffy!

Pickles always loved bath time and she happily stood in the tub while I scrubbed her with shampoo until she was gloriously fragrant. After I had rubbed her dry, I brushed her coat and trimmed down her feathery legs and along her belly, finishing with snipping her fringe. Then I cut her nails, which she tolerated, and brushed her teeth, which she didn't. Carefully, I wiped around her beautiful eyes and swabbed inside her little ears.

'Pretty as a picture!' I told her when I was done. Gypsy came nosing onto the patio, where I had been finishing off the pampering, and sniffed Pickles with suspicion, as if to say: 'Why do you smell so weird?' Pickles simply tossed her newly neat hair and bustled off into the kitchen, like a proper little diva.

'It's Pickles's big day tomorrow,' I told Gypsy, rubbing her back. 'Do you remember your first time on a film set? Lots of fun but very tiring, so we need to make sure she has a good rest tonight.'

It was a beautiful warm evening, so I sat out in the garden as the sun went down, lazily tossing a ball for the dogs. As usual, Pickles shunned the game in favour of sitting curled in my lap. It took me right back to that first night, when I brought her home and she had demanded to sit up on the sofa with me instead of in the bed I had made her. I smiled; she had been so weak and poorly, but she had always known her own mind.

I could hardly believe how far Pickles and I had come together – despite a few bumps in the road. What seemed like an impossible journey when we first started out had led us all the way here, with Pickles fully trained and about to take her first steps on a movie set.

As always, I felt nervous about starting the film, but also excited to show off my little dog, of whom I was so proud. Her time to shine had finally arrived.

Chapter Twenty

Girls on Film Set

The arrival of the big day was heralded by my alarm sounding at 5 A.M. Days on set start notoriously early, and I still hadn't quite got used to the dawn wake-up calls. But I was up and out of bed without the need for my usual ten-minute snooze that day, the adrenalin waking me up more effectively than any coffee.

Pickles was back in her rightful place at the end of my bed, and I could see her working hard to drag herself from sleep. She watched me with bleary eyes as I got up, as if to say, 'Do you have any idea what time it is?'

She perked up when I served her breakfast, though. After she had eaten, I took her on a short walk as the sun came up, conscious that I didn't want her too hyper when we arrived at the studios. In the breaking dawn the fields were covered with a golden haze, and I had a feeling it was going to be a good day.

Back at the cottage I spent about five minutes getting myself ready – a fresh pair of jeans and a quick lick of mascara – then got down to the real business of making Pickles look like a film star.

Ever obedient, she was as good as gold as I gently brushed her coat – which by now was a gorgeous chestnut colour – until it hung smooth and straight. Then I gathered up her fountain-like fringe in a topknot and secured it with a pretty lilac bow. She certainly looked the part.

As usual, Pickles was lapping up all the attention, but of course she had no idea what the day had in store for her. I wanted to keep her as calm as possible so packed her pink blanket in the crate with her before we set off for Pinewood Studios. Jo would be round later to look after the other dogs.

'Today's the day,' I told Pickles, catching her eye in the rear-view mirror. 'Your silver-screen debut – but don't be nervous, you're going to blow them away.' Pickles watched me attentively, but I was chattering away to calm my own nerves as much as hers.

With the roads clear at this early hour, we were at the studios in no time. I have been lucky enough to shoot many movies at Pinewood over the years, but I still get a thrill from heading there for a job. The sprawling complex is Britain's answer to Hollywood – known as the home of James Bond and host to all sorts of iconic British productions, from *Chitty Chitty Bang Bang* to the *Carry On* films.

A typical day starts with exercising the animals and getting them familiar with their surroundings, before I and any other trainers I'm working with go for a much-needed coffee. Then we will go on set to find out exactly what is required that day. There is often a lot of waiting around so I use that time to train the animals or just play with them, so they don't get bored. When we are called on set for our scenes I will take instruction from the director on exactly how he or she wants to position the animal, then I will either stand off camera or occasionally be in shot in costume – somewhere the animal can see me giving the commands. Generally, each scene needs to be shot multiple times from various angles, so we repeat it a few times before taking a break.

There's always a good period at lunchtime for us to exercise the animals and grab some of the delicious food from the catering truck. Generally, there's no finish time given – you're just there until the director has got the shots he needs.

I always try to make it as relaxed and as fun an experience as possible for the animals, but the first day can be a bit of challenge. There's a lot of new things for them to get used to – and it would be no different for Pickles.

We pulled up in the car park just before 7 A.M. and I was barely out of the car before an officious-looking young woman, dressed all in black and with the obligatory headset strapped on, was by my side.

'Julie Tottman and Dog?' she asked. Then, without waiting for a response, 'Right this way please.'

'You heard her, Dog,' I joked to Pickles. The runner was already striding off without a backwards glance. With one hand I grabbed the enormous bag of stuff that I had packed to keep Pickles happy during a day on set, and with the other I tugged gently on Pickles's lead.

We followed the stern woman in black through the hubbub of the early-morning film set, which can only be described as organised chaos. Sets are far bigger than most people imagine, sprawling across several acres on which scenes will be built and dismantled in a matter of hours. Cables snake across the ground and golf buggies carrying cast or crew rush around like *Wacky Races*. This morning there were builders banging some complicated-looking bit of scenery together, and riggers hooking up their enormous lights. Extras dressed incongruously in fancy garden-party attire milled about, while a small army of black-clad crew in headsets barked orders at them. There was a maze of trailers for the cast and crew, and I could smell the catering truck, cooking up the morning bacon rolls. Noisy and busy and full of new sights and smells – the film set was a long way from the peaceful farm back at Long Marston.

But when I glanced down at Pickles, I saw her trotting confidently at my heels, just like she always did. Her ears were pricked forward and her eyes darting about, taking everything in. Every few seconds she would look up at me as if to check I was OK with it all too. I smiled to myself – she was loving it, as I had hoped she would.

The runner showed us to the small trailer that would be ours, unceremoniously marked with a sign reading 'DOG'. She gave us a curt nod and disappeared without another word.

I clambered up the steps and let us into the trailer, which I would describe as bijou if I was being charitable – or tiny, if I wasn't. There was just enough room for a small brown sofa and a fold-out table, plus a counter with a kettle and toaster. You don't get anything fancy if you're not Brad Pitt.

I unloaded Pickles's bowls from my bag and gave her some water, which she lapped up happily. 'It's a glamorous life, isn't it?' I asked her as I searched in vain for a light switch.

Once I had unpacked our stuff, I clipped Pickles back onto her lead and took her for a short walk around the edge of the studio complex. Usually, if you keep away from the main set there's plenty of places for a dog to run and play, which is important when we are there for so long.

We had only been back at the trailer five minutes when there was a knock at the door. I opened it to find Nick, one of the assistant directors. There are typically about five of these on a movie, working under the main director, and the first assistant tends to be the person who tells us what is needed and what the animal is required to do. Nick was my main point of contact on this film, to whom I had been sending progress reports on Pickles. Luckily, he was also a dog lover.

'Hi, Nick!' I said brightly. 'Have you come to check on your newest cast member?'

'Absolutely,' he grinned, stepping inside. 'I couldn't wait a moment longer.'

He crouched down on the floor and started making a fuss of Pickles – although, like a true pro, he was careful not to ruffle her artfully arranged hairdo.

'Listen, Julie, there's been a bit of a change to the schedule,' he said. 'We've decided to kick off today with the Queen's garden party. The weather isn't

154

looking good for this afternoon so we want to get it in the bag while we can. Is that OK?'

I hesitated. It wasn't really a question – on a movie set, what the director says goes. It's not like they're going to change their schedule because a lowly animal trainer isn't too keen on the plan.

But it wasn't ideal. The original schedule had been for Pickles to do some shots in the arms of her on-screen owner, the actress Sylvia Syms, during scenes with her co-stars Colin Firth and Anna Chancellor. I had been relieved to see this because it would be a nice way to ease Pickles in, getting her used to the lights and cameras, as well as Sylvia, before she had to do anything more complicated.

In contrast, the garden party was one of the most difficult scenes she had to pull off. The idea was that Pickles would jump from Sylvia Syms's arms, then run through a crowd to Amanda Bynes, where she would sit up and beg – just as we had practised behind the village hall all those weeks ago. To do all that on a film set, with a crowd of new people, was a lot to ask of a little dog who was only just getting used to her surroundings.

But when had Pickles ever decided that something was too much of a challenge?

'Sure, that will be fine,' I told Nick as he straightened up. 'But I was wondering – do you think I could be in the scene too, so I can stay close to her?'

'No problem,' he replied. 'You better get yourself down to wardrobe!'

Chapter Twenty-One

Action!

Getting into costume is not something I do if I can avoid it – I much prefer being hovering off camera than in front of it. But, given that this was going to be a big crowd scene with lots of distractions, I wanted to be able to be by Pickles's side, and that meant I would have to blend in with the extras.

An hour later, I was trussed up in a peach cocktail dress and heels, my hair twisted into a complicated updo under a wide-brimmed hat – all courtesy of the rather miraculous wardrobe department, whose trailer, stuffed full of outfits for any eventuality, was just a short walk from mine. Pickles, used to seeing me in jeans and wellies, looked up at me doubtfully. 'Oh, stop it,' I muttered. 'I know I look weird – I don't need you to remind me.'

From wardrobe, we headed to the prop department – always important for me to get acquainted with, as they supply anything the dog will be wearing – and picked up the diamanté collar that Pickles needed for the scene. I had no sooner got that round her neck than our runner was hurrying us towards the main set, where the director and his assistants were busy assembling the extras playing guests at the Queen's garden party.

Rain might have been forecast for later but for now the sun was shining gloriously, the perfect conditions for the scene. Across the sweeping lawn, marquees, Union Jacks and a red carpet had been laid out, and you really could believe you were at Buckingham Palace.

Action!

Like me, the other extras were all in their finery, the women in pastel two-pieces and wide hats and the men in smart three-piece suits. It always takes quite a while for the director to be happy with how everyone is positioned and lit, but finally the stars were brought on set. They always come on last, so they don't have to wait around as much.

I caught sight of Amanda Bynes being led to her mark – a vivacious brunette with a megawatt smile. She was only seventeen but by the way she was chatting away to the crew I could tell she was a seasoned pro; after all, she had been a TV star since she was a child.

While I was craning my neck to spot Amanda, I hadn't noticed that Colin Firth, dashing in a grey pinstripe suit, and Sylvia Syms, in an extravagant lilac hat, had also taken their positions.

Pickles and I were taken over to them as Pickles would start the scene in the arms of Sylvia, who was playing Princess Charlotte, a fictional relative of the Queen.

'Aren't you gorgeous?' exclaimed Sylvia.

'She knows it too,' I joked, carefully brushing a stray hair from Pickles's eyes.

Pickles was as friendly as ever with her new owner, although I did feel a slight pang as I put her into Sylvia's arms. My baby was on her own now. 'Do me proud,' I whispered to her as she fixed me with that soulful stare. 'I know you will.'

I took my place in the crowd, just a few feet away from where Sylvia, with Pickles hugged against her chest, would film her lines with Colin. Pickles swivelled her head round to look at me, but when I gave the signal she turned back to look at Sylvia, just as we had practised with Jo.

My heart was in my mouth as I surveyed the assembled crowd. Even though we had rehearsed with the villagers back home, there were far more people here. A crowd is always such an unpredictable environment; you have no idea what might distract your animal or throw them off. I remembered how manic Pickles had been that day behind

160

the village hall and prayed she would show some more focus today.

Then suddenly I clocked the Steadicam approaching. It was a camera on an enormous rig, which looked like a great metal dinosaur. A cameraman explained to me that when Pickles ran through the crowd the Steadicam would run along after her, capturing the moment. I gulped. That all sounded a bit much for a little dog filming her very first scene. I hoped Pickles wouldn't decide it was a frightening predator and run away.

When at last the director had everything positioned as he wanted, the clapperboard came out and he called, 'ACTION!' Stomach churning, I locked my eyes on Pickles and told her, 'Jump!'

Right on cue, she leapt from Sylvia's arms, and suddenly she was running through the crowd like her life depended on it. And oh, the expression on her little face as she ran! Her mouth was spread right open in the biggest smile, and every step she took was a joyful leap. I had to fight the urge to whoop and cheer as my little dog flew through the air as if she was delight personified.

I was overwhelmed before Pickles even got to Amanda Bynes, but then she hit her mark perfectly and was straight up onto her haunches, begging with her eyes twinkling, and I burst into floods of tears.

When I thought back to the fragile little terrier I had first met three and a half months ago, crippled with disease and a stranger to human kindness, it was hard to believe this was the same dog. She was radiating happiness and you would think she had done ten film jobs before. I could hear people murmuring, saying 'Isn't she good?', and I thought my heart might burst with pride.

The script said that Amanda Bynes was meant to ignore Pickles, but I could see her really struggling to resist the urge to bend down and give her a good pet. As soon as the director called 'Cut!' the actress did exactly that. I was properly sobbing by this point, so much so that the welfare nurse, on set to look after everyone's health and emotional needs, came hurrying over.

'Are you all right, dear?' she asked. 'Has something happened? Do you need to have a little sit down?' She was looking at me like maybe someone I loved had died.

'Oh – no,' I hiccupped through the tears. 'I'm not crying because I'm sad – I'm happy ... I'm just ... just – so proud of my dog!'

I pointed at Pickles, who was now rolling on the floor as Amanda and Colin fussed over her, soaking in all the praise and attention like she was born for it.

The nurse looked puzzled. 'Has she been having trouble with this scene?' she asked.

'Oh, it's not that,' I sniffed, the tears of joy still rolling down my face. 'This is actually the first time she's shot it ...'

With me gabbling nonsense through my tears, the nurse evidently decided that I did need to sit down after all. She pulled up a chair and bustled me into it, while I jabbered away about how Pickles had been rescued from an illegal puppy farm.

'That's interesting,' said the nurse kindly. 'I'd have thought a dog like this would have been born and bred for a movie set!'

I had to laugh at that. 'This is her first time! I wasn't certain she would make it: she was a death's door when I got her ... but just look at her now.'

As if she knew we were talking about her, Pickles abruptly picked herself up and came galloping back towards me, leaping into my outstretched arms. I hugged her close, not even caring that my tears were making her carefully groomed hair all soggy. 'I'm so proud of you,' I whispered to her. 'You are the star I always knew you would be.'

The nurse had produced a pack of tissues, which she handed to me. 'Now I'm welling up too!' she said. 'What an extraordinary story – if you hadn't told me, I would never have guessed your dog hasn't been doing this for years.'

I felt almost giddy with the emotion of it all.

Action!

Right from the start I had known Pickles was clever and brave – but to see her prove it to the world was something else.

Pickles had come through the worst and out the other side. And she and I were a team. Together we had done what seemed impossible just a few months ago. Nothing could make me prouder, or happier, than that.

Chapter Twenty-Two

A Star is Born

Pickles loved her first day on set from beginning to end. The crowd scene was shot several times so the director could get it from multiple angles. Each time I called 'Jump!' to Pickles she did her run even better than the previous time, and she knew it. As soon as they called 'Cut!' on each take she would look around her as if to say, 'Why are we stopping?' Then she would start bouncing around excitedly, knowing she would be getting lots of cuddles and treats.

A *Star is Born*

The weather was still holding out at lunchtime and I was able to enjoy my delicious chicken and mushroom pie on the benches outside. On most of the films I had worked on I had been with other trainers, so it felt unusual to be by myself today. But I didn't really mind because I had Pickles for company, and a text from Glenn waiting on my phone, asking how it was going.

After taking Pickles for another walk around the studio grounds, it was back to the set for some close-ups of her in Sylvia's arms. The camera loved her, and she loved the camera – I could see her preening, tilting her head this way and that as if to say, 'Get me from my best angle!'

'What a little diva,' joked the cameraman. 'Seriously, though, they say never work with children or animals but when you meet a dog like this one you wonder why.' I almost started crying all over again at that.

When it was finally time to go, Pickles was worn out – and so was I. But I felt completely elated by how well the day had gone. Pickles snoozed all the way home, but I was bursting to talk to someone about how brilliantly she had performed.

Jo, who was busy training animals for a run of adverts we had booked in, was waiting for me at my cottage when I got home. I poured us both a big, cold glass of celebratory white wine.

'I wish you'd seen her, Jo,' I said. 'She was honestly smiling – you've never seen a dog so happy!'

'That's brilliant, Jules,' she told me. 'It's testament to you – so many people would never have taken a chance on a dog like Pickles, but look at how it's paid off.'

'Well, it was touch and go for a bit, wasn't it? Thank God my second-in-command never let me give up!'

Pickles got lots of cuddles that night, which was no less than she deserved after everything she had achieved that day. Then we both needed an early night, with another full-on day ahead of us tomorrow.

A Star is Born

The next morning, when the alarm sounded at 5 A.M., Pickles pinged awake and was excitedly licking my face before I had even switched it off. 'All right, all right,' I said, rubbing my eyes and sitting up. How the tables had turned in just twenty-four hours. Pickles would barely stand still as I brushed her coat, and I could tell she was itching to get back to work.

When I pulled up on set that morning, I noticed something had changed. The same black-clad woman was waiting for us, but her stern look had been replaced by a sugary smile. 'Hi, Julie!' she simpered. 'How is Pickles this morning?'

Well, there was no end to Pickles's talents: she had even managed to turn this slightly intimidating person into goo. Then I started to get suspicious – what had changed? Were we in trouble?

'My name's Esme, by the way,' said the runner as she rubbed Pickles's belly.

'Wait, how do you know Pickles's name?' I asked

Esme. As far as I knew, she was still 'Dog' to everyone but me.

'Oh, everyone knows about Pickles,' said Esme
warmly. Now I really started to worry – were we
going to be fired?

'Such a sad story,' Esme went on. 'It's really
amazing what she's overcome.'

The penny dropped. It seemed that ever since
my emotional breakdown in front of the nurse
yesterday, tales of Pickles's rough start in life had
spread like wildfire.

I suddenly found that I had a mini celebrity
on my hands. While the actual celebrities – the
film stars – were respectfully ignored, everyone
wanted a piece of Pickles. I can't say I minded: it
was lovely to have so many engineers, cameramen,
runners, even cast members seek us out to make
a fuss of her.

Generally on a film set, the crew members I work
directly with are limited to the director and assistant directors, the prop department and sometimes

170

the art department, who book us if the dog is just going to be in the background. But I always end up meeting all sorts of people, like the grips, who are responsible for all the technical elements of the lighting; the drapesman, who dresses the set; and the script supervisor, who makes sure there are no continuity errors between scenes, because they all want to have a cuddle with whatever animal I have brought along.

Pickles, now used to people making a fuss of her wherever she went, was in her element.

While she lapped up the attention, I never doubted that Pickles would get distracted from her work, because she had eyes only for me. That devotion never wavered, and however many people came to hug her – and no matter how famous they were – I knew she was always my dog.

A small audience had gathered to watch Pickles shoot her scene for the day, which would involve Amanda Bynes 'teaching' her to roll over. The set was done up as a grand ballroom, with oil paintings adorning the walls and elegantly dressed extras gathered to play the attendees at a fashion show.

Amanda had to take Pickles from Sylvia's arms, then start playing with her. Pickles was meant to pretend not to know how to roll over, then eventually do it under Amanda's instruction. I wasn't worried about the part where she got it right – but I feared she might be too much of a show-off to act like she couldn't do the tricks she had already perfected.

As usual, she didn't put a foot wrong. The scene was one we had rehearsed over and over up at the farm, and Pickles made it look effortless.

'Are you sure it's this dog's first film?' Nick, the assistant director, said to me at the end of the day. 'She hits her marks better than some of the actors.'

'Well, I guess you can't bribe an actor with ham,' I laughed. Everything was going perfectly – but I knew there was still a big challenge to come.

Chapter Twenty-Three

Going Out with a Bang

We spent nine days on set, without a single wobble. But I was nervous about Pickles's final scene. It was to be filmed on location at Halton House, a grand country mansion in the Chiltern Hills. While Pinewood had become like a second home for Pickles, this was going to be another new environment to get used to.

That didn't bother me much, but the scene itself was potentially problematic. The setting was a grand ball, and Pickles was to sit in the arms of

Anna Chancellor while an enormous chandelier plunged from the ceiling and smashed into pieces.

All she needed to do was remain completely calm – which should have been easy. But it was still less than a month since she had been attacked, which had left her jumpy when it came to loud noises.

Jo and I had discussed the problem before filming had started, and we had come up with a creative solution. Pickles wasn't really the main focus of the scene, so we could get away with having a stuffed toy as a stand-in. I knew a brilliant prop designer, and had commissioned them to make a replica Pickles. I had carried her fluffy double in my bag since day one, just in case of an emergency. I had never had any call to use it – yet.

The evening before the Halton House scene, I talked it over with Jo.

'I really don't think we will need the stuffy,' I said. 'I know Pickles was getting frightened of loud noises before but there's been all sorts of weird sounds on the set and nothing has fazed her. I know the shot will look better if Pickles is in it rather than a toy – even if the only person that notices is the director.'

'Well, you're the one that knows her best,' said Jo. 'If you think she'll be OK, then do it. But just remember, the chandelier is a very expensive prop and they can only smash it once!'

'That's what's bothering me,' I admitted. I knew the chandelier must have cost an arm and a leg. 'But she's done everything else perfectly first time – why should this be any different?'

As I drove to Halton House the next morning, I still hadn't decided what to do. Pickles was curled happily in her crate, and stuffed Pickles was packed carefully in my bag. I knew what my preferred option was – but was it worth the risk?

The morning's filming went like clockwork, with Pickles required to film some scenes where she was passed between Sylvia and Anna Chancellor. As usual, she was laid back, comfortable and seemingly having the time of her life. It made up my mind: she was doing the chandelier scene.

At lunchtime I gave her a big cuddle and then groomed her coat again, retying her hair in its cute little topknot. 'It's time for the big finale, Pickles,' I told her. 'All you have to do is keep calm and carry on – you can do that, right?' She licked her nose and held my gaze. That was good enough for me.

The ball scene had an enormous cast – Colin Firth, Amanda Bynes, Anna Chancellor, Christina Cole and Eileen Atkins were all in it, as well as a couple of hundred extras. They were all assembled in a lavish, twinkling ballroom, dressed to impress, as a live band played. I was reassured to see that Pickles wasn't thrown off by the noisy band; in fact, she seemed to be rather enjoying their rendition of James Brown's 'Get Up Offa That Thing'.

Above all of it glistened the enormous chandelier. It wasn't real glass – the magic of prop design meant that when it smashed it would look like it was, but without the dangerous side effects – but you would never have guessed. With twenty-four candles and dripping in (imitation) crystal beads, I could tell it was going to make quite a crash when it came down.

In the film, Amanda Bynes's character is at a stuffy debutante ball and decides to liven up proceedings by getting the band to play the James Brown song and encouraging everyone to start dancing. The heavy bass makes the room start to shake and the inevitable happens: the chandelier smashes to the floor, much to the displeasure of the host, Lord Orwood, played by Roger Ashton-Griffiths.

As Jo had reminded me, the chandelier was indeed very expensive, and there was palpable tension in the air as the director got everyone into position. There would be only one chance to get it right, so there was to be a run-through using an empty barrel as a stand-in. The prop master had rigged it up to a complicated pulley structure, and everyone was primed to give their best shocked faces the moment it dropped.

'OK, people!' yelled the director. 'Let's see what you've got.'

The cameras weren't rolling so no one shouted action, and everything happened much quicker than I expected. Momentarily distracted by a runner who was trying to nudge past me with a coffee for one of the assistant directors, I didn't have my eyes on Pickles as the barrel came clanging down. It seemed to take her by surprise too, and suddenly her shrill little bark was ringing through the set.

'Can we get the dog trainer on here to stop that racket?' shouted the director, exasperated. I was already hurrying towards Pickles, who was trying to squirm out of Anna's arms. As soon as she saw me, she settled down, and I knew her momentary panic had only been because she hadn't been able to catch my eye for reassurance.

'Is she going to play up?' the director asked me.

'If there's any chance she's going to mess up this scene I would rather she wasn't on my set.'

'Oh, no, I promise she'll be fine,' I said, and as I spoke I somehow knew it was true. 'Just a little mishap – it won't happen again.'

The director frowned but resumed his station by the monitors. The cast were back in place; it was time to smash the chandelier.

This time, I was taking no chances. I positioned myself just off camera, as close to Pickles as I could get, making sure I was directly in her eyeline so I could hold her gaze.

'Right, people, this is a one-take scenario so let's get it right!' called the director. His assistant counted down: 'Three, two, one … ACTION!'

My heart was in my mouth as the prop master released his rope and the chandelier hurtled to the ground. *CRASH!* Every ounce of me willed Pickles not to react. Fragments of fake glass exploded everywhere, glittering in the studio lights. The cast jumped back as the camera panned to their astonished faces. And Pickles never took her eyes off me. I saw her flinch as the crash came, but apart from that she didn't move a muscle. 'Stay,' I was whispering. 'Stay. Good girl. That's it. Calm.'

'Aaaaand cut!' called the director. I felt the air rush out of me in a huge sigh of relief. The risk I had taken had paid off. In fact, Pickles was so chilled out about the whole thing that I saw her having a massive yawn as I hurried over to retrieve her.

'Well done,' said Anna Chancellor as she handed Pickles back to me. 'Don't worry about the run-through. You've trained a really brilliant dog there: she jumped less than me when the chandelier came down.'

'I might have trained her, but it's all down to her really,' I smiled. 'She's pretty extraordinary.'

And that was it – Pickles's last scene was a wrap. I felt quite emotional as I loaded her back into her crate for the final time. The end of every job was always a bit like that. It meant the end of an era, during which you had spent every moment of every day with a particular animal, getting to know what makes them tick and building a relationship where you can communicate implicitly. After all that time living and working alongside them, it feels weird to finally have achieved what you set out to do all those months ago.

But this job was extra special. Not only had I pulled off the first movie for Birds & Animals UK without a hitch, I had done it with Pickles. To see her thriving and happy after the horrors she had endured was an emotional high like no other.

I knew it was what would keep me going with this job, not just with Pickles but with other rescue animals like her. Playing a part in this sort of transformation was why I put up with the 5 A.M. starts, the crazy filming schedules, the demanding directors and all the other stress that comes with making movies. There's simply no other feeling like it.

I had just finished packing up the car when I

saw Esme running towards us. 'Julie!' she called, out of breath. 'Thank goodness I caught you. The director wanted me to give you this.'

She handed me a handsome leather jewellery box. I opened it to find a pink leather collar with a circular pendant, engraved with the name Pickles. I turned it over. On the back it read 'What a Movie Wants'.

Esme smiled. 'He said she was the best dog he's worked with.' I couldn't help it. I grabbed Esme and pulled her into an awkward hug – mainly so she couldn't see I was crying, again.

Chapter Twenty-Four

Home Truths

It's always strange going from the buzz of a film project to the reality of everyday life. But after everything that had happened recently, I was grateful for the return to normality.

The next couple of weeks were a chance for Pickles – and me – to catch our breath. As usual, the time spent intensively training and then away on set had caused me to neglect my paperwork, and there was a dispiriting mountain of the stuff for me to make my way through now that I had some time on my hands.

I made sure that I still fitted in training sessions with Pickles every day. She didn't need them, but a dog doesn't understand why training would come to an end just because a movie has; for them, it's just a fun routine. Just as I do with all my dogs, I needed to keep Pickles busy and make her feel as important and loved as ever. It was one of my favourite parts of the day. Pickles made me laugh every time – once, I taught her how to crawl along on her belly, and after seeing my ecstatic reaction when she got it right she spent the rest of the day slithering around the house.

'Pickles, you don't have to do it all the time,' I giggled. 'Even though it does look very elegant . . .'

Business was good, and I was trying to get used to the feeling of being the boss. The feedback from *What a Girl Wants* had been excellent and the Birds & Animals UK diary for the rest of the year was filling up with TV work and adverts. It finally seemed like the risks I had taken were paying off.

But there was a question hanging in the air, which I was refusing to confront. What would happen to Pickles next? I knew the sensible answer: she needed to be rehomed.

Usually, the animals live with me while we are preparing for a project, then when filming wraps I foster them with trusted friends, knowing I will still be able to use them for future filming as and when I need to, but also that they will have a lovely family life. They are still mine – I pay for their food, their vet bills and anything else they need – and ultimately, they are my responsibility. I always make it a condition that if for whatever reason it doesn't work out, which has never happened yet, the animal returns to me.

I already had four dogs living with me, and the next project was going to require me to house and train three more. Deep down I knew it was time to start looking for a foster family for Pickles – but I couldn't bear the thought of being parted from her.

It was Jo who brought it up in the end. We were

sitting in my garden one late-summer afternoon, and I was throwing a ball for Pickles, who had that delighted little smile on her face as she tore after it.

'So, I know it's going to be difficult but . . . have you thought about who might take Pickles now the film has ended?' Jo began, tentatively.

I sighed. Of course, I knew this conversation was coming – but that didn't make it any easier.

'Well, as you can imagine I've been trying not to think about it at all,' I admitted. 'But I do know I can't put it off for ever.' I took a deep breath, before continuing, 'Do you remember my friend Liz, who rehomed Daisy, from *102 Dalmatians*? I said I'd keep her in mind for a dog because Daisy passed away last Christmas. She could be an option for Pickles.'

'Liz would be great,' said Jo gently. 'She was brilliant with Daisy so you know she'd give Pickles a wonderful home. And doesn't she live just a few miles away? You'd be able to pop round and see Pickles all the time.'

These were all things I had told myself already, but I could feel tears pricking my eyes as I thought of Pickles being a short drive away, rather than happily curled at the end of my bed.

'I know you're right, Jo,' I said, burying my head in my hands. 'But I just don't know how I will ever say goodbye to Pickles.'

'I know,' she said, putting her arm round my shoulders, and I leaned my head against her. 'There's no rush. Just something to think about.'

Over the next few days, I thought about almost nothing else. Somehow, I just couldn't picture my cottage without Pickles. I knew that the next movie project was going to take up a lot of my time, and with the new dogs set to arrive I needed to think about space. But on the other hand, Pickles was so closely bonded with me. She had already suffered so much loss and trauma in her life, would she really be as happy anywhere else?

A few times, I picked up the phone to dial Liz's

number, then put it back down. There was something holding me back.

To distract myself, I had some professional portraits of Pickles taken – a bit like the headshots you'd see of an actor. I do this for all the animals I think could go on to other projects. Pickles had been such a little star on *What a Girl Wants* that I hoped she would be able to book more work – mainly because I knew how much she would enjoy it.

Of course, being a little diva, the day out at the photographer's studio was a treat in itself. While some dogs will go wild in a studio, sniffing around all the lights and cables, she arranged herself like a supermodel, striking pose after pose for the laughing photographer. I was delighted with the results, which really captured her livewire personality.

With those pictures posted on my website, there really was no other reason to put off the decision about what to do with Pickles. And yet still I was torn. My head said one thing, but my heart quite another.

Chapter Twenty-Five

A Walk to Remember

I was still wrestling with the decision over Pickles's future home as Glenn and I walked over the hills beyond the village one Sunday in early autumn. By now this was one of our rituals; he had come on so many walks with me and the dogs now that even his allergy seemed to be getting a bit better. As we walked, we would talk about anything and everything, switching easily between deep questions and silly jokes. I was starting to feel like I knew him inside out, and it was getting harder and harder to keep a lid on my feelings for him.

It was my favourite time of year, when the trees started to turn. I loved to see the golds and russets of the autumn leaves, and the blackberries budding on the hedgerows. There was a gentle breeze with just a hint of the chill which was to come, and the low sun cast long shadows.

With Glenn by my side and the five dogs playing together up ahead, I felt a sense of deep contentment washing over me. And I knew that had a lot to do with Pickles – the scene simply wouldn't be the same without her. I decided to see what Glenn's take was regarding what I should do.

'I don't think I can part with Pickles,' I told him, after I explained the situation. 'The plan was always to get her well, do the movie, then find her a new home. But I can't imagine my life without her now.'

Glenn looked at me, shocked. 'You can't let go

of Pickles!' he said. 'She worships you – I've never seen a bond between dog and owner like it.'

'I know. And I'm just as attached to her as she is to me. It's one of the reasons I'm so reluctant to re-home her.' Pickles dropped a tennis ball at my feet, which I bent to throw for her.

'Look, Jules, it's all very well having plans, but that doesn't mean you have to stick to them religiously. If you feel like you should keep Pickles, you should keep her. She's only tiny – how hard can it be?'

We both looked back at Pickles, who, during the course of the walk, had burrowed through a hedgerow and jumped in several puddles, so now had twigs stuck in her hair at jaunty angles and mud up to her elbows. As usual, she had a happy smile on her face as she tore back and forth, trying to catch up with the other dogs. She was going to need some serious cleaning up when we got home, but she was a little ball of joy – and it was infectious. Glenn caught my eye and we both laughed.

'Sometimes the heart trumps the head, I guess,' I said. 'Thank you – for helping me see things clearly.'

Glenn and I walked on in companionable silence as I turned the idea over in my mind, clambering up the last steep part of the path to the crest of the hill. Of course he was right: I was *always* going to keep Pickles. She needed me and I needed her. Suddenly it seemed like madness that I had even considered finding her a new home. We belonged together.

When we reached the top of the hill, the view was truly spectacular. The golden autumn sun was turning the sky pink in places and casting the valley below in a buttery glow. The villages dotted along the roads which stretched to the horizon looked tiny from up here, as did the sheep grazing in the fields like little puffs of cotton wool.

'Isn't it beautiful?' I exclaimed, turning to Glenn. But he wasn't looking at the view at all. He was watching me, with a strange look on his face.

'Julie—' he started, then stopped himself and took a deep breath. I felt my heart start to race as he continued.

'Listen, if we're talking heart versus head stuff – I don't want to do anything that's going to ruin our friendship. But I really think you should know . . . I'm falling for you.'

I felt suddenly dizzy, like I hadn't just reached the top of the hill but had jumped soaring into the pink sky. It's what I had been longing for him to say, ever since the day I met him – and here he was, on this perfect evening, making all my dreams come true.

I couldn't speak, so I just took a step forward and kissed him. He circled his hands around my waist, pulling me closer, and it felt like the world stopped spinning just for us.

When at last we pulled away, his handsome face seemed at once totally familiar and brand new. I could hardly believe this moment was real.

'In case you couldn't tell, I'm falling for you

too.' He laughed and took my hand as we walked giddily back down to the village, unable to believe our luck that we'd found each other.

So just like that, there on the hillside, Pickles got a forever home and I got a boyfriend. Sometimes you just have to listen to your heart.

Chapter Twenty-Six

What Pickles Did Next

From that moment on, Pickles's place in my life was never questioned again. She was very talented as a performing dog, but she was even better as a pet. I couldn't have asked for an animal who was more devoted or loving. From the moment she woke up in the morning – at the end of my bed, of course – she would stick to me like glue, watching me always with those soulful eyes.

If I ever left her in the cottage, even if just to pop to the shop for some milk, as soon as I arrived home she would be going mad, squealing with delight to see me again, bouncing up and down to demand a cuddle and wagging her tail so hard it looked like it might fall off. It was quite the reaction – and it never stopped me feeling like the most special person in the world.

Mostly, though, I just took her with me wherever I went. She was so little I could tuck her under my arm and off we would go. She was basically a celebrity in the village and neighbours would rush out of their houses to greet me as we went by. Keen to see how their contribution to her training had paid off, many of them had gone to watch *What a Girl Wants* when it came out. I was constantly being grilled about life on set, or what Pickles was going to do next. Although a lot of my neighbours – especially the women – just wanted to chat about Colin Firth, which was quite understandable. I had to tell them it was more than my job was worth to tell them anything too detailed – but I could confirm he was just as handsome in the flesh.

I had been to see the movie too and was delighted with how it had turned out. Of course, I was biased, but I thought Pickles stole the show. Jo and I had gone to watch it in a busy cinema and there was an audible 'awww' after Pickles's big moment at the garden party. I was glowing with satisfaction like a proud parent, and had to stop myself from tapping other cinema-goers on the shoulder to say, 'That's my dog!'

Watching the film got me thinking that I must find another part for Pickles. She was so good, it would be a shame not to let her talent shine. I was really busy, training other animals for a number of upcoming projects as well as building up my contact base for Birds & Animals UK. But there had been lots of requests for dogs to play smaller parts and I knew one of them had to be right for Pickles.

I chatted it over with Jo as we wrangled four greyhounds we were training up at the farm. It was much slower progress than it had been with Pickles – the dogs got distracted by any small movement in the distance and would often tear off at a hundred miles an hour, leaving us to helplessly run after them, shouting.

As we caught our breath after one such sprint, I asked Jo if she thought any of the jobs we had booked would be a good fit for Pickles.

'What about that dog food advert?' she said, wiping sweat from her forehead. 'They said they want a range of different breeds and they seem pretty openminded about what, but they did specify that one of them had to be a little dog.'

'Yes, but they said they wanted the little one to be scruffy!' I said indignantly. 'My Pickles isn't scruffy.'

Jo laughed out loud at that. 'Have you seen Pickles lately?' she said. 'Most of the time her hair's all over the place, her tongue's hanging out and who knows what's hiding behind her ears. I know you think that because she once played a princess's pet she's a princess herself, but it's a long time since she looked like royalty.'

'Jo!' I exclaimed in mock horror. 'Yes, I may have to admit I have my rose-tinted glasses on when it comes to Pickles, but she will always be a princess to me.'

'Well, I'm sure she's not too grand for a dog food ad,' joked Jo. 'Have a look at the job spec tonight – they want us to send a selection of options by the end of the week. If you think you can bear for her to slum it with the commoners, we can put her forward.'

That evening when I got home, I tried to look at Pickles from an objective point of view. To me, she was the most beautiful little thing in the world. But taking a step back, I had to admit that Jo had a point. While she was still glowing with health, her hair did indeed stick up in random tufts no matter how often I brushed it. There was a cheekiness about the way she cocked her head to one side and despite her airs and graces she was definitely still that scrappy little fighter from the puppy farm.

'What do you think, Pickles?' I asked her. 'Reckon

you could pass for scruffy?' She popped up onto her hind legs to beg, something she knew would always get a smile from me. I laughed. 'You don't care as long as you get the chance to show off, do you?'

The dog food ad required a gang of five different dogs, led by a bearded collie. Jo had already started work with the collie, who would break into a safe to get at the dog food. A scruffy little dog would press a button to switch off the security lasers, allowing the gang to make a clean getaway. It sounded cute, and I knew Pickles would be able to pull off the tricks required. I wrote back to the advert producers, attaching her headshot along with those of the other dogs I thought would be perfect to work alongside her.

Just a few weeks later we were arriving on set, Pickles having secured the role of scruffy sidekick. The crew had set up an elaborate-looking vault in the studio, though the lasers would be added in later by special effects. Jo's collie was to be the face of the dog food brand, and had already spent a day filming lots of close-ups and having his photo taken with boxes of food. I wondered how Pickles would feel about having to play second fiddle.

In the end, I don't think she even noticed that she wasn't the star of the show. She and the other dogs were beside themselves with excitement when they realised they would be required to do multiple shots where they would be gobbling dog food. Talk about a dream job!

'You'd think they had never been fed before!' joked Jo as we watched the dogs delightedly licking yet another bowl clean.

Her collie made all his scenes look effortless – she had even taught him to drive a getaway car – or at least pose in the driving seat with his paws on the wheel – which was just the cutest thing. I knew Pickles would be just as good: I had spent ages teaching her to push buttons and flick switches. In fact, I was glad the switches in my house were out of reach, or I fear she would have spent all day turning them on and off.

She was raring to go when it came to her scene, and smashed her big red button perfectly. 'Clever girl, Pickles!' I told her again and again, as the camera crew shot the scene from various angles. To Pickles, it made no difference – Hollywood movie or dog food commercial, she was happy as long as she was performing and getting all the fuss and attention she deserved.

The advert producers were delighted with how all the dogs had performed, and Jo and I couldn't keep the smiles off our faces as we loaded our canine stars back into the cars to travel home.

Once we were back at the cottage, Pickles was still bouncing around, full of energy – she just loved to be in front of the camera. I vowed I would find her plenty more opportunities for her to do what she did best.

Little did I know that she was about to reveal talents I didn't know she had. A chance encounter would put her to the test in ways I could never have expected.

Chapter Twenty-Seven

Out in the Cold

After the success of the dog food advert, I knew Pickles would continue to pick up film work. She was a little star – and now she had both princess's pet and scruffy urchin on her CV, she had proved how versatile she was too.

Glenn was spending more and more time at my place, battling bravely against his allergy to dog hair. He was particularly fond of Pickles, who always demanded he made plenty of fuss of her no matter how much he was sneezing at the time.

Thankfully, she also seemed to have suffered no long-term trauma from her terrifying encounter with the snarling dog and would no longer hesitate, whichever route through the woods I chose. Looking back, I marvelled that I had ever been worried. After everything Pickles had already overcome, she wasn't going to let some nasty rogue dog turn her into a quivering wreck.

In fact, I had almost forgotten about that dog and its mysteriously silent owner. Before *What a Girl Wants* had started filming, when I was so worried about Pickles, I was obsessing every day about the attack and what I would say to the young man if I ever saw him again. But so much had happened since then that, these days, I barely gave it a second thought. Since that afternoon on the farm when we had glimpsed him in the distance, I had not set eyes on him again, so it felt safe to assume neither he nor his dog were worth worrying about any longer.

Then, one midwinter afternoon, we unexpectedly

came face to face with Pickles's attacker. But I could never have imagined what would happen next.

I had been in London that morning, having a meeting with a TV production company who were hopefully going to sign an important contract for Birds & Animals UK to supply animals for a number of their upcoming dramas. Jo was looking after most of my dogs in my absence, but Pickles was so small and well behaved I had simply popped her in my handbag and taken her with me. She loved riding the escalators and going on the Tube, taking it all in with big round eyes.

The meeting was a success – not least because all the execs were charmed by Pickles. I had told them her story and explained how she epitomised my philosophy about rescue animals. When I left – much sooner than I expected – I had guaranteed work from them for the next two years.

The early finish meant that Pickles and I arrived back at Tring station not long after lunch. I wasn't due to pick up George, Ginelli, Gypsy and Lala until around five, and it was a beautiful afternoon, so I decided we should take advantage of it. Instead of picking up my car and turning back towards the village, Pickles and I headed into the hills on foot.

The air was cold but crisp, with the stark branches of the trees in dazzling focus against the bright icy blue of the sky. If only all winter days were like this, I thought, squinting against the brilliant sunshine. Pickles trotted along quite happily, kept cosy by the little purple jacket I had dressed her in that morning. At this time of year, if you saw the sun you had to get out in it, no matter how chilly it was.

I was so lost in my daydreams and the beauty of the day that I barely paid attention to where we were going. I clambered over stiles, following the yellow footpath signs along a route that was not familiar to me. This is what country life is all about, I told myself happily, enjoying the simple pleasure of getting comfortably lost in the wilderness.

We followed a winding stream, but then the

path suddenly ran out where the river had burst its banks. 'Damn it,' I said to Pickles. 'It's flooded – I don't think we can go on.'

I considered turning back and retracing our steps, but time was getting on and I knew we needed to head back towards the station as quickly as possible, before it got dark. I sensed that we could cut the corner off and rejoin the original footpath if we took a shortcut over a field. It wasn't something I would usually do, but I guessed the farmer wouldn't mind, considering the normal route was impassable.

Tucking Pickles under my arm, I climbed over the fence and into the overgrown field. At least there are no crops or livestock here, I thought – I wouldn't have wanted to cross if there were.

It was then that I heard a dog bark – and it didn't sound friendly. In fact, it sounded positively threatening. My heart beating fast, I quickly scanned the horizon. There, at the edge of the field, was a dog – one that looked awfully familiar.

In my arms, Pickles gave a scared little whine. 'Don't worry, baby,' I told her. 'You're safe with me.' I started to back towards the fence, keeping my eyes on the dog in the distance. It was weird that it hadn't come bounding over. Something didn't feel right. Somehow, the fact that it hadn't was even more scary – what was wrong with it?

I started to climb back over the fence, and from that elevated viewpoint I could see the dog properly. Suddenly I realised why it had stayed away: it was chained to a stake hammered into the ground.

'How strange,' I said to Pickles. Who would come all the way out here to chain up a dog and then just leave it? I wasn't sure if the dog was one who had attacked her, but even if it was, it was potentially in trouble. And I could never walk by an animal in distress. I sighed – there was only one thing for it.

Approaching very cautiously, I drew closer to the dog. It looked healthy enough, but why was it out here on its own? The dog watched me warily, a low growl in its throat, and I could see the tension in its powerful muscles. But I spoke in a gentle voice, holding my hand out towards him so he could see I wasn't a threat. 'Good boy,' I murmured. 'We're not going to hurt you. It's OK.'

Under my other arm, Pickles remained remarkably calm. Her little nose was twitching, but she never panicked. I felt a rush of pride for my brave little warrior. But what on earth was I going to do about the dog?

'Oi! What are you doing?' A voice rang out. I spun round, and saw the same pale-faced boy I had first encountered on the day of the attack emerging from the corner of the field. So I had been right – this was the dog that had pounced on Pickles. The boy was dressed in dirty tracksuit bottoms and a thick black coat, a checked scarf wrapped so tightly around his head that I could only just make out his features. His battered trainers were caked in mud.

'Oh, I didn't realise anyone was here,' I

stammered. 'I thought the dog had been left on his own. I was just trying to help.'

'Well, don't,' said the boy, harshly. I saw his gaze travel from my face to the little dog under my arm, and a flicker of recognition, before his face snapped to a perfect blank again.

All the severe speeches I had rehearsed in the aftermath of Pickles's ambush, ready to deliver to this guy if I was ever to find him, seemed to have disappeared. Now that I saw him up close, I realised he was much younger than I thought he was – probably only in his mid-teens. Instead of anger, I now felt only confusion. What on earth was he doing out in this remote field?

'You know this isn't a public footpath?' I asked him now, more gently. 'It's probably not a good idea to stop here too long – the farmer won't be pleased.'

'It's none of your business,' said the boy. I saw his eyes flick nervously to the corner he had emerged from, and with a shock I realised there was a tent there, partially hidden by low-hanging tree branches and undergrowth.

'Wait . . . are you camping out here?' I said before I could stop myself. 'It's so cold! Do your parents know you are here?'

'Oh, piss off,' said the boy. 'I told you: mind your own business.' He was furiously unlooping the chain tying the dog to the post. I couldn't believe he was out here in this weather – could he really be sleeping here? Several large bags of rubbish were scattered close to the tent, which suggested he had been there for some time, and a scorched patch of earth as if he had recently lit a fire.

The boy yanked his dog after him and stalked away from me, back towards the tent. I stood there watching him go, a knot of worry gathering in my stomach. He was barely more than a child and he was out in this remote spot, all on his own, with the temperature set to dip below freezing. Surely he couldn't really be living here? Maybe this was just somewhere he came to get away from his parents?

Reluctantly, I headed in the opposite direction, knowing I had to pick up my pace if I was going to get to the car before dark. I hated to leave the boy and the dog, but what could I do? He had made it quite clear he didn't want my help. Pickles strained in my arms, trying look back over my shoulder. It was as if she too was wondering what on earth we had just witnessed.

Chapter Twenty-Eight

Field Research

My mind was still whirring when I got back to the station car park. I picked up the Shogun and drove over to Jo's. Her home was always so warm and welcoming, and with a dog or cat curled in every possible corner. With my five as well, it was a bit of a madhouse.

Jo had made lasagne for dinner and was chattering away as she served it up, but I could barely follow what she was saying. I had so many questions about the scene I had stumbled upon today, and none of the possible answers seemed good.

'Earth to Jules!' I was jolted out of my thought spiral, and immediately felt guilty that I had been so distracted.

'What's going on with you?' Jo asked. 'I don't think you've said two words since you got here.'

'Sorry, Jo,' I sighed. 'It's just I saw that boy today – you know, the one with the dog that attacked Pickles?'

'Really?' exclaimed Jo. 'Well, I hope you gave him a piece of your mind, nasty, irresponsible thug that he is.'

'Not exactly.' I told her about the tent, and how dirty and uncared for the boy looked, and the dog chained to a post, as if they weren't just passing through. As Jo listened her expression went from exasperation to one of concern.

'So you think he's all on his own?' she asked when I had finished. 'And he might have been out there for a while?'

'I think so, maybe,' I replied. 'But I don't know what to do. I thought about calling the police, but I just have a feeling that something is going on with him, and potentially getting him into trouble for trespassing isn't going to help matters. I think I've got to go back there tomorrow.'

Jo considered this for a moment. 'Well, I'm coming with you, then,' she said. 'And if he still refuses to talk, then we'll have to get the police involved. Agreed?'

I nodded. 'I just hope that when we go back, there's no sign of him and I was mistaken about the whole thing. There's probably a perfectly innocent explanation for it all. I hope I'm worrying over nothing.'

'You probably are, Jules.' Jo smiled reassuringly. 'Still, it's good to be certain.'

As I left that night Jo promised to pick me up first thing in the morning so we could drive back over towards the place where I had seen the boy.

I was still worrying about him when I got into

bed that night, and I am certain Pickles could tell. Instead of taking her usual spot at the foot of the bed, she snuggled up in the crook of my arm. As I stroked her pretty little head, something told me I should take her with us tomorrow. Pickles was the key to cracking this particular mystery – I just wasn't sure how.

There was a frost on the ground when I woke the next morning, shimmering in the early dawn light. Shivering as I got out of bed, and pulling on thick leggings and a fleece, I dreaded to think how cold sleeping outside would be. I hoped the boy's tent was just a den he hid out in when he wanted some space to himself, that I would be proved wrong about his sleeping arrangements.

Jo and I had planned to head back to the field really early. Our hope was we wouldn't find him, proving that he didn't in fact stay there overnight. Now that I'd had chance to sleep on it, I was convinced this would be the case. I told myself I was probably worrying about nothing.

I was ready and waiting for Jo when her grey car pulled up outside, and hurried out to meet her, Pickles under my arm.

'What are you doing with Pickles?' she asked incredulously.

'I'm bringing her with us,' I answered. 'We should make it look like an innocent dog walk, right? But it will be too chaotic with the bigger dogs.'

Jo, wrapped up warmly in a parka and bobble hat, looked at me doubtfully. 'Are you sure you want her near that dog again?'

'She's not scared at all,' I insisted. 'In fact, I know it sounds crazy, but I think she could help.'

'OK, if you say so . . .' said Jo, unconvinced, as I strapped myself in.

Under my instructions, Jo drove us as close as we could get to the path I had followed beside the river the previous day. She parked up and I led her along the riverbank, until we reached the bit that had been flooded.

'No option but to climb over the fence, I'm

afraid,' I said. I could feel butterflies rising in my stomach as we clambered into the field. Would the boy and the dog still be here?

There was an eerie silence as I desperately scanned the edges of the field, hoping against hope that they would be empty. I was already planning to buy Jo a 'sorry I wasted your time' breakfast when I heard a dog bark.

My heart sank. It was the fierce dog, which I could now make out in the early-morning gloom. Which probably meant his owner was here too.

Chapter Twenty-Nine

Lost and Found

'Don't worry, the dog is chained up,' I told Jo. We approached slowly, and I could see the tent was still there. There was no movement from inside.

'Hello?' I called out. 'Are you there?' Silence. Jo and I looked at each other.

'We're here to help you,' I said. 'Please come out.' Nothing.

Jo cleared her throat. 'Well, Julie, if no one's here I guess we will have to call the police,' she said loudly. *That wasn't part of the plan!* Then she winked at me, and I realised what she was doing.

'Er, yes, the police,' I played along. 'They're going to be pretty interested to hear that someone is trespassing. And if this dog is abandoned, I imagine they will have to send it to a shelter.'

Suddenly, there was a commotion as the tent was zipped furiously open. The boy's face, his nose red with the cold, appeared. 'Don't call the police,' he said desperately. 'I can't lose my dog.'

'Hello again,' I said, and I could see his annoyance when he saw it was me.

'What on earth are you doing sleeping out here?' chimed in Jo. 'You could catch your death!'

The boy's face clouded over with anger, and he yanked his head back inside the tent. I put my hand on Jo's arm. 'Leave this to me,' I whispered.

Carefully, I approached the tent and crouched down at the entrance. Inside, there was a tangle of blankets and clothes. The boy wouldn't turn to look at me.

Gently, I put Pickles down and she started to sniff at the tent. I knew she would see a turned back as a challenge, and sure enough, she trotted over to the boy and licked his hand. Startled, he pulled his hand away, but then he paused. Pickles was staring up at him with those big brown eyes, and he seemed to soften. Reaching out his hand, he ruffled her hair. She gave a delighted little shimmy.

'I think she likes you,' I said. The boy turned to look at me. 'I'm Julie,' I said, trying to make my smile as reassuring as possible.

'I'm sorry about what happened before,' he mumbled. 'I should have had Duke on the lead – I would never want to hurt your dog.'

'That's OK. Sometimes dogs can do unpredictable things. I'm sure Duke isn't a bad dog.'

The boy's face brightened. 'He isn't. He can just sometimes be a bit overprotective. But he's good as gold with me.'

'You obviously love him a lot. I can understand that – Pickles here is one of the most precious things in the world to me. But aren't you worried about him spending the night out here in the cold?'

The boy was immediately defensive again. 'He sleeps in here with me,' he said crossly. 'I just let him out for the toilet when it gets light.'

'So you are sleeping here, then,' I said, and I could see him register his mistake. 'How long have you been doing that? And why?'

I could see him wrestling with whether to tell me or not but, sitting at the entrance to his tent, I had him cornered, in more ways than one. As he weighed it up, he turned back to Pickles, tickling her chin and giving her a pat on her belly.

'Give her a cuddle if you like.' He hesitated, then pulled her onto his lap and she snuggled into his chest. 'See!' I told him. 'She's a proper little fan of yours.'

Holding Pickles like a protective shield seemed to give the boy confidence to speak. 'I ran away from home,' he said in a rush. 'My mum's new partner – all he does is yell at me and threaten me all the time. He doesn't want me there. And my mum does nothing. I had enough, OK?'

He was looking at me defiantly, as if daring me to say he was wrong to have run away. I was aghast at his story, which was even worse than I had expected. By the sound of it, he wasn't just blowing off some teenage angst but fleeing a seriously bad situation.

I tried to keep calm and think about what I needed to ask next. From his accent, it sounded like he had grown up in London, not rural Hertfordshire.

'That must have been really hard for you,' I said. 'But is there really nowhere else you can go? No adults you can talk to about this?'

The boy made a sound of disgust. 'My uncle lives near here,' he said in a flat voice. 'I stayed with him in the summer and I liked it. When I left home I went straight to him, but he didn't want to know.'

There was a silence which I resisted filling, sensing that if I was patient he would reveal more. Pickles gave him an encouraging lick on the hand.

The boy sighed. 'When I turned up on his

doorstep my uncle was really angry. He said I couldn't stay, and I should stop making my mum's life hell. So I just ran off. I snuck back later because I knew he had a tent in his garage, and I nicked it. Then I tried to find a place no one would find me. I've only been out here a few days, honest.'

I was horrified he had been out for several nights, in this icy weather. But, conscious that I didn't want him to see my alarm, I tried to keep my expression neutral. 'What have you been doing for food?'

He looked guilty. 'I nicked that too,' he said, his eyes flicking to the rubbish bags full of empty crisp packets and chocolate-bar wrappers. 'But I'm running out now.'

'You know you can't stay out here,' I said. 'I am going to have to tell someone where you are.'

The boy looked panicked again. 'I can't go back to my mum's. It's awful there.'

I looked back at Pickles, who was quite content

in his arms. She had fled trauma and abuse too – and all she needed was some TLC. I knew what I had to do.

'Listen, why don't you come home with me for now? You can warm up – have a bath. I'll make you something to eat. Then we can decide what to do after that.'

The boy shook his head fiercely. 'No. I'm fine on my own. I don't need your help.'

I sighed. 'You must realise you can't stay out here in this weather. I'm offering you a lifeline here. Do it for Duke's sake, at the very least.'

He paused and looked down at his hands. I held my breath. 'OK,' he mumbled. 'But don't get me into trouble.'

'Lovely,' I said brightly. 'Let's get all this stuff packed up then. My friend Jo is here too, we can help.'

The three of us made short work of folding up his battered two-man tent and gathering up the rubbish bags. As we worked, the boy revealed his

225

name was Michael and he was seventeen. As I had guessed, his mum's flat was in north London.

'She must be very worried about you,' said Jo.

Michael gave a hollow laugh. 'I doubt it,' he said. 'All she cares about is her boyfriend now.'

We were quiet as Jo drove us back to my house, Pickles on my lap, Duke squeezed into the footwell of Michael's seat, at his insistence. I was struggling to process the revelations of the morning, and wondering what on earth I should do next.

Back at the cottage, I ran Michael a bath, as promised. Without his hat and coat he was a gangly, slightly built kid with close-cropped dark hair. It wasn't even 9 A.M. but he said he really wanted to eat a jacket potato and beans, so I put that in the oven for him. I could tell he didn't really trust me yet, but he had instantly bonded with Pickles – and that seemed to be enough to convince him to stay.

As he wolfed down his breakfast, I raised the question of his family again. 'Don't you want to give them a call, let them know you're all right?' I asked.

He rolled his eyes. 'I told you, my mum won't care.'

'You might be surprised,' I told him. 'And what about your uncle? He must be worried too.'

Michael said nothing. 'You know I'm going to have to get the police involved, and social services,' I said gently. 'I'm just an animal trainer, I can't sort this out on my own.'

This piqued his interest. 'You train animals? Can you help me train Duke?' he asked.

'I'd love to,' I said. 'We can do a session this morning, if you like. But you have to call your mum first.'

'Fine.' Result, I thought, as I fetched the phone. I made myself scarce so Michael could talk to his mother in peace. When I was certain he had finished, I knocked on the kitchen door. Michael opened it, his eyes rimmed red. All his swagger was gone, and he looked like a lost little boy. He needed a hug, but I knew he would pull away from me.

I could feel Pickles fussing around at my feet, so I picked her up and put her into his arms. He buried his head in her fur, and I knew it was the right thing to do. If anyone understood how Michael was feeling right now, it was Pickles.

Chapter Thirty

Amazing Pickles

Events moved fast after that. It turned out Michael's mother had indeed been worried sick and had reported his disappearance to the police. Sadly, runaway seventeen-year-old boys from council estates, who have been on the wrong side of the law before, are not exactly a top priority.

Michael's uncle Jim, a gruff bachelor who lived a village away, blamed himself for what happened. He wasn't a bad man, he was just exasperated by what he perceived to be Michael's constant troublemaking. When Michael turned up on his doorstep Jim had, by his own admission, flown off the handle. After all, Michael was no angel and had given his mum the runaround over the years. She had been on her own for so long – why did Michael have to kick up a fuss about her new man? But Jim had no idea how bad things had really got between Michael and his mum's new partner, who sounded like a nasty piece of work.

The fact that Michael had chosen to camp in a remote field in the middle of winter, rather than return home, was a wake-up call for all of them. His mum wasn't prepared to break up with her boyfriend, but it was clear he and Michael could not continue living under the same roof. So Jim asked Michael if he would like to move in with him instead.

I was relieved that the worst-case scenarios had been avoided. Michael didn't have to return to live with the man he hated, and nor did it become a complicated social services issue. Plus, by the sounds of things, it was a good idea for Michael to get out of London and away from the bad crowd he had fallen in with since leaving school. Once he moved in with Jim, he got on to a carpentry course at a local college, and found a job in one of the pubs in the area.

He and I stayed in touch, mainly because he wanted me to help him with Duke, who his uncle had agreed to let move in too. As I had suspected, Duke wasn't a bad dog. He had some aggression issues, which had surely been exacerbated living in a small London flat amid a volatile environment. But he was loyal to Michael and could be sweet and affectionate, in the right mood.

I worked with Michael on identifying Duke's triggers, how to anticipate them and manage his behaviour. With lots of long walks, more social-isation with other dogs and exercises to keep his stress levels low, Duke turned into a much calmer pet.

Glenn popped over to the cottage one evening

just as Michael was leaving after a training sessions. Michael was saying his usual goodbye to Pickles, crouched on the floor to give her lots of attention, which she lapped up in her normal open-hearted way. As I waved him and Duke off, I realised Glenn was watching me with a funny look on his face.

'You put a lot of faith in people, Julie,' he said. 'That boy and his dog almost killed Pickles last year. Not everyone would have been able to get over that.'

'What, you think I shouldn't have forgiven him?' I said, annoyed. 'You know how much he's been though – once I knew his story it was pretty hard to blame him.'

'No, it's not that!' Glenn exclaimed. 'It's actually pretty amazing. You see the potential others can't see.'

I flushed pink. I never saw myself as anything special. But I supposed it was pretty amazing really. Who could have predicted all those months ago, when Pickles was attacked, that I would one day get rather attached to her attacker?

But then, when Pickles was involved, extraordinary things seemed to happen. It had been my little dog who had first broken the ice with Michael. She had been his comfort in the hardest time. And now she even played happily with Duke, proving that there is nothing you cannot overcome if you have a little courage.

Yes, I did put my faith in people – but I had put my faith in Pickles first.

Pickles's support of Michael through his crisis suggested that in another life she would have made a great therapy dog. She had a special skill for seeming like she was really listening, and lavished gentleness and affection on those that needed it most. But at heart she was a performer, and I kept putting her forward for film work because that was where she was at her happiest.

It wasn't exactly a struggle – the jobs just kept rolling in for her. As is often the way with film work, someone who worked with you on one project remembers you the next time they need a dog and gets in touch. Pickles starred in all sorts, from period dramas to kids' TV, often as a 'dressing' dog. Cast by the art department, these roles call for a dog who isn't a central character, so isn't required to do much other than stay in position and look cute. Not exactly a challenge for my gorgeous Pickles.

One of my favourite parts was in *Amazing Grace*, a film about William Wilberforce and his role in abolishing the slave trade. It had a fabulous cast – Ioan Gruffudd as Wilberforce, Benedict Cumberbatch as William Pitt and Romola Garai, Rufus Sewell and Michael Gambon all starring as well. There were lots of dogs in that film, meaning plenty of trainers too, so it was a fun, sociable few weeks. Pickles's part wasn't very demanding – she was a background character, playing a pet dog – but the attention everyone gave her was something else. Having dogs on set can do that sometimes:

they become a focal point for the cast and crew, and anyone who wants five minutes away from the stress of it all will turn up at the dog trailer, desperate for a cuddle.

Pickles was always delighted to be picked up and made a fuss of, and was totally unfazed by being passed around and cooed over by strangers. If it's possible for a dog to have charisma, that's what she had in spades. She had the ability to make you feel like she understood your innermost thoughts and would never judge you for them.

Most film dogs retire at about eight or nine, but Pickles showed no signs of slowing down. She came alive on a film set, like it was her natural habitat. And she never got bored or frustrated with training; she was always as keen to learn a new trick as she had been when I first started training her. It never occurred to me to call time on her film career because it just made her so happy, and her good health meant it was easy to overlook the fact that she was getting on in years.

The longer I had her, the less I thought of her as a puppy-farm dog. That all seemed like a distant memory now, and I liked to tell myself Pickles had more or less forgotten those awful years of cruelty and neglect. Sadly, the legacy couldn't be completely undone – and a souvenir of her time on the puppy farm was about to rear its head.

Chapter Thirty-One

Hollywood Smile

Pickles had come to me with so many health problems, and I was proud to say that she overcame most of them. But there was one area where it was already too late to make a big difference: her teeth.

The poor diet Pickles had been fed during the formative years of her life had caused numerous infections in her gums. Yorkshire terriers are prone to teeth issues as it is, with 80 per cent of them likely to suffer dental disease by the age of two. This starts with tartar build-up, which if not addressed can cause gum infections. Bad diet can make this even worse. Of course, the cruel puppy farmers wouldn't have cared a jot about Pickles's dental health.

By the time Pickles came to live with me, when she was about five, she was already riddled with dental problems. Right from the start I would regularly brush her teeth – much to her horror. While she accepted almost everything else without complaint, Pickles couldn't abide the twice-weekly ritual where I would poke around in her mouth with the toothbrush as she did her level best to wriggle away. 'It's for your own good,' I would soothe her, giving her lots of little breaks because I knew how stressful she found it. 'You'll thank me in the long run.'

I meant it too – I knew just how important oral hygiene is for dogs. Dirty teeth cause bad breath and swollen gums, and if an infection gets in it can potentially spread around the body, causing damage to the kidneys, liver, heart and joints. After the precarious position I had found Pickles in, I wasn't going to take any risks. And if that meant she had to endure the slightly unpleasant process of my brushing her teeth, then so be it.

I also booked her in for an annual deep clean at the vet's, during which she was put under an anaesthetic so Michelle could carry out a proper scale and polish, a bit like humans have at the dental hygienist. It was a routine procedure that Pickles had for several years without complaint.

When she was about ten, I arrived at the surgery to pick up Pickles after her deep clean. I was expecting to meet a nurse, who would hand her over, but instead found Michelle waiting for me. She asked me into her consulting room, where she stroked Pickles's head gently.

'What's all this about?' I asked, worried. 'Nothing went wrong, did it?'

'No, not at all,' reassured Michelle. 'Pickles is as strong and healthy as ever. But we do need to talk about these teeth. I'm sure you've noticed how much worse they've got this year.'

I sighed. Recently Pickles had been struggling with her dry food, so I had been feeding her lots of soft food instead. 'I know,' I said. 'I'm trying my best and brushing them even more regularly. But it doesn't seem to be making much difference.'

'You've done a great job, Julie,' said Michelle. 'But you're right – it's not making much difference any more. And neither is our clean and polish.' She gently peeled back Pickles's lips so I could see inside her mouth. 'Look here – these teeth on the side. They are really rotten. I don't think there's anything we can do to hold back the tide.'

'What does that mean? Will she have to have them out?'

Michelle nodded. 'If we don't remove the worst teeth it's going to affect all the others and cause her a lot of problems. I'd say we could just step up the cleaning regime but that's going to stress her out, and we don't want her having too many anaesthetics now she's getting older.'

It gave me a bit of a shock to hear Michelle

describe Pickles as 'older'. She still had the energy and spirit of a much younger dog, so I rarely thought of her advancing years, even though I knew in dog years she was entering old age. Accepting that we needed to take her age into account meant admitting that maybe I didn't have too many years left with her. I felt a lump in my throat at the very thought.

Looking back down at my little dog, I knew that agreeing to the operation was the right thing to do. Those bad teeth were only going to get worse if we didn't act, and I knew that dental infection could cut a Yorkie's life by as much as three years. Even so, it would mean a substantial operation, and would affect how she could eat and digest her food for the rest of her life.

'If you recommend we do this, then let's do it,' I told Michelle.

Michelle smiled. 'I know she'll be just as cute without her teeth.'

I booked Pickles in for her operation the

following week. I felt strangely emotional as I drove to the surgery, knowing that I would have to leave her there overnight. It felt like a line in the sand. When I had first rescued Pickles, we had got her well with time, love and a refusal to give up. Now she needed proper surgical intervention. I hoped it wasn't a sign of things to come.

'Take good care of her,' I managed as I handed her over to Sally, one of the nurses. 'I'm already counting down the hours until I get her back!'

'She'll be back by the fire with you before you know it,' smiled Sally. 'Don't worry about her, Julie, we do this operation all the time.'

The whole day felt very strange without my little shadow by my side. It probably wasn't a good idea, but I found myself Googling canine dental extraction. It's a much bigger procedure than it is for a human to have a tooth out. Dogs evolved as hunters, meaning they have very strong teeth to catch their prey, and deep tooth roots as a result. Surgical extraction sometimes requires the gum and bone to be cut to remove the tooth, then reconstructed afterwards. Poor Pickles!

The next morning, when it was time to pick up Pickles, I was outside the surgery before it even opened. I couldn't wait to get her home. Michelle had text me to say the procedure was a success and Pickles was recovering well, but I was desperate to see her for myself.

When Michelle arrived to unlock the surgery, she laughed to see me already waiting. 'You're keen!' she said. 'Let me just check in with the nurse who has been here overnight, then I'll be right back with Pickles.'

I sat nervously in the waiting room, and then jumped up when I heard the scrabble of little feet approaching. 'Pickles!' I cried, opening my arms wide. Michelle let go of Pickles's lead and she sprinted towards me, jumping up into my arms. She certainly didn't appear to be traumatised by the surgery.

She was wriggling around so much I wasn't able

to get a good look at her, so settled for letting her nuzzle happily into my neck.

'Come through,' said Michelle, and I followed her into her examining room, putting Pickles onto the table.

'Do you notice anything different?' said Michelle tentatively. That's when I suddenly clocked it: Pickles's tongue was lolling out to one side. She looked so funny – like a little alien.

'Well, she's certainly not got a Hollywood smile!' I joked.

'Not exactly,' smiled Michelle. She gently peeled back Pickles's lips again, so I could see the empty spaces where six of her teeth had once been. 'She's just getting used to the new feel of her mouth, so she might poke her tongue out like that for a few weeks. Hopefully she will go back to normal once it has all completely healed.'

'Oh, I don't mind. I actually think she looks kind of cute – and it's certainly a USP to put on her résumé.'

Over the next few weeks, we settled into a routine not dissimilar to those very first few days when I brought Pickles home from the puppy farm. I would curl up by the fire with her and stroke her head, and she absolutely revelled in the nursing she received. I liquidised her favourite foods – adding in some special bits like steak or chicken thighs – and she loved that even more.

'I think you quite like being a patient, don't you?' I asked her. 'Don't get used to it – I want you back to full health as soon as possible.'

It wasn't long before she was, but that tongue remained stubbornly poked out to one side. I couldn't get over how funny it made her look. She certainly didn't have any regal dignity left – she was a proper little jester now, with the silly expression to match.

When Jo popped over to see how she was getting on, she got a fit of giggles. 'Oh, come on, Jo!' I said, trying to suppress a laughing fit myself. 'She's still beautiful to me.'

Jo managed to catch her breath, wiping tears of mirth from her eyes. 'She's very beautiful,' she hiccupped. 'But she also looks exactly like a Furby!'

I dissolved into giggles then too – Jo was spot on. With her bat-like ears and big round eyes, Pickles had always had a passing resemblance to the furry robot toy, but now, with the slightly deranged look her tongue lolling out gave her, she was the spitting image. I didn't care, though – it only made her cuter, in my eyes.

Amazingly, Pickles new look didn't stop her picking up work. She kept booking jobs well into her teens, and directors seemed to love her unique appearance. Every time I thought about retiring her I would see the energy and enthusiasm with which she approached any day on set, and decided against it. I think she would have been happy to go on for ever if she had the choice. Sadly, fate had other ideas.

Chapter Thirty-Two

The Impossible Question

When I first met Pickles, close to death after her horrendous five years on the puppy farm, I would never have believed she would go on to live longer than any other dog I had ever owned.

But then Pickles had always been full of surprises. By the time she reached twenty, I had become convinced that she would simply live for ever. Even at that grand old age, she still had the energy and lust for life of a much younger dog.

She was queen bee of the household by then,

always bagging herself the comfiest spot on the sofa and demanding that she was the first to be fussed when I got in through the door. She was the most solid thing in my life, a loyal little presence who was as loving and reliable throughout all the change that fifteen years can bring.

Then, one evening, she didn't finish her dinner. That was unusual – Pickles had maintained a hearty appetite, even without her teeth, and usually licked the bowl clean. I didn't worry at that point; sometimes even the greediest dogs are simply not hungry.

But the next morning, she managed just one mouthful of her breakfast. Now I became concerned. She had started to lose weight over the past fortnight or so, but I put that down to old age. If she was turning her nose up at food as well, it was time to get the vets involved.

I packed Pickles into the car and took her on the familiar journey to see Michelle. As always, Michelle was delighted to see my little dog – she

always said Pickles was one of her greatest success stories.

'Hello, Pickles!' she exclaimed, but I saw her face
drop when she saw how much more subdued Pickles
was than normal. Pickles gave a half-hearted wag
of her tail as Michelle checked her over.

'Hmm, no obvious signs as to why she's stopped
eating,' said Michelle, peering into Pickles mouth.
'I'll give her an injection that should stimulate her
appetite, and we'll see how it goes.'

As I tucked Pickles back into her crate I was
taken right back to that first visit here all those
years ago, when she had first arrived from the
puppy farm and was struggling to keep food down.
Back then, Michelle had assured me Pickles was a
fighter. I hoped it was still true.

I kept an eye on Pickles over the next couple
of days, but she was still unwilling to eat. Her
energy levels had dropped noticeably, and instead
of engaging with my other dogs she curled herself
up on her own. I could feel the panic rising in my

stomach. Surely nothing serious could be wrong, I asked myself. It's Pickles – she's immortal!

Back we went to the vet's, where Michelle told me they would have to keep Pickles in for some further tests.

'Bye-bye, baby,' I whispered to Pickles as I prepared to leave her with Michelle. 'I'll be back for you very soon – be brave, OK?'

'She's in safe hands,' said Michelle kindly. 'I'll ring you around five with the test results.'

It felt so wrong, returning to my car with an empty crate. I hoped Pickles wouldn't think I had abandoned her. I comforted myself, knowing that Michelle would take the best possible care of her. It was just like that time with her teeth, right? A few tests, some treatment and she would be right as rain.

I spent the rest of the day watching the clock, waiting for Michelle to call. I knew she wanted to run various blood tests as well as do X-rays and a scan. Maybe Pickles had just eaten something she shouldn't have, and it was blocking up her gut. I didn't want to consider any other possibilities.

Just after five, the phone rang. I leapt to pick it up on the second ring.

'Hi, Julie,' said Michelle. 'Listen, we've got the results from the tests back – but I think you'd better come in to the surgery, and I can fill you in properly.'

That didn't sound like good news. I felt sick as I drove over to Wendover Heights, terrified of what Michelle was going to tell me. But I was excited to see my little Pickles too – it had only been a few hours, but I missed her already.

When I arrived at the vet's, I only had to look at Michelle's face to know that my worst fears were justified. She was pale and serious – which could only mean one thing.

Pickles, meanwhile, perked right up when she saw it was me, bouncing up and down on her ancient little legs. I picked her up and gave her a big cuddle, trying to choke back my emotions.

'Hello, gorgeous girl,' I murmured. 'Did you miss me as much as I missed you?'

'Julie,' said Michelle. 'You've probably worked out that it's not good news.'

'I figured, yes,' I sighed as Pickles snuggled into my chest. 'I'm ready – just tell me how bad it is.'

Michelle took an intake of breath. 'The scan showed a tumour. And it's quite advanced. As we both know, Pickles is a little trouper, so although she's probably been ill for some time it's only now, when it has got quite bad, that she's started to let on.'

I could feel my vision go blurry as I ruffled Pickles's hair. That was just like her, to carry on as if everything was fine while a poisonous growth was sapping her energy from within. She would do anything to make sure the people around her were as happy as possible.

'Is there anything we can do?' I managed.

'Well, we could operate. Cut the tumour out, and that could be the end of it. But it's a big operation, which at her age she might struggle to recover from. We can't be certain that it would cure the cancer either, so it's a bit of a risk.'

I knew what Michelle was saying: the operation would potentially extend Pickles's life by a couple of months, but at twenty years old, which was already unusually good for a dog, was it really worth it? I stroked Pickles's head gently, and she stared back up at me, those deep brown eyes full of love.

'You don't need to make a decision now,' Michelle was saying. 'Take her home, think it over, and let me know what you'd like to do. We'll support you, whatever course of action you choose to take.'

'Thanks, Michelle,' I said, and leaned over to give her a hug. 'You've been a great vet, and a great friend to us too.' Michelle gave me a weak smile and brushed something away from her eye. I could tell that delivering this news had been tough on her – even though she must see so many sick pets and distraught owners, I doubted it ever got any easier.

As I drove home, Pickles curled up in her crate, I considered the operation. On the one hand, I thought I'd do anything I could to squeeze out a few more months with Pickles. But on the other, surely that was a selfish way of looking at it? Pickles would have to stay at the vet's overnight, have a general anaesthetic, then undergo major surgery. If she survived it – and we couldn't rule out the possibility that it would prove just too much for a dog of her age – she would face an uphill struggle to recover. Could I really put her through all that, just because I wasn't ready to say goodbye?

Chapter Thirty-Three

Time to Say Goodbye

By the time I arrived home, I had made up my mind. As an animal owner, the last and most important thing you can do for your pet is give them a comfortable end. And for Pickles, that meant not subjecting her to the surgery.

That evening, I sat on the sofa with Pickles on my lap, stroking her ears, just as I had done for years and years, ever since she first arrived here covered in mange and dirt. I still had her pink blanket from the rescue centre, and I tucked it

WILL YOU TAKE ME HOME?

around her now so she was extra cosy. She made the same little contented sighs as she got herself comfortable. Tears rolled down my face as I thought of a future without this precious little dog in it. But no matter how badly my heart was breaking, I knew what I had to do.

The next morning, I rang Michelle and told her that I would not be going ahead with the surgery.

'I think it's the right decision,' she told me. 'The chances of the operation making any significant difference are so small compared to the risks involved. It will be much easier on Pickles this way.'

'How long have I got left with her?' I asked, trying to keep the tremor out of my voice.

'It's hard to say,' said Michelle gently. 'It could be as much as a year, or it could be just a few weeks. You'll just have to keep an eye on her. If she takes a turn for the worse, or seems to be in serious discomfort, bring her down to the surgery.'

She didn't need to fill in the blanks – I've had enough dogs put to sleep to know that when the time comes, it's up to you to know when to act. I hate playing God, but I would never want an animal of mine to suffer.

I had four more months with Pickles, in the end. Her appetite perked up a bit and I made sure that whatever she wanted in that time, she got. For my little diva that meant smoked salmon, prawns and sushi were all on the menu. She was tired all the time, so spent a lot of her last days snoozing in her favourite spot on the sofa, and when it was time to go out into the garden I carried her there to save her little legs. I showered her with love and attention, determined to make her feel as special as she deserved.

All the while, I watched her like a hawk, knowing that if she showed signs of further suffering I would face an awful decision. Eventually, it got to a point where she stopped eating again, and was reluctant to go outside to the toilet. I knew her quality of life was ebbing away, so I phoned Michelle and told her it was time.

It's still a hard memory for me to recall even now. I can remember the seemingly endless journey to the vet's, during which questions swirled in my head – was I doing the right thing? Could I have done more? I can remember taking Pickles into Michelle's room and hugging my friend, whose eyes were already rimmed red. And I remember stroking Pickles's paw as the injection went in, and my tears falling on her auburn fur as the life in her slowly slipped away.

'Goodbye, gorgeous girl,' I whispered to her. 'I'll never forget what you taught me about love and determination. I'm so proud of everything you have achieved. Thank you for all you have given me, my beautiful baby.'

Over the years I've had to go through this horrible ritual with all sorts of animals, all of whom have been precious to me and all of whom I have grieved for. People say it must get easier, but it really doesn't. It's not something you can ever get used to, and it hurts just as much each time. When it's a dog as precious as Pickles, the pain can be almost unbearable.

Afterwards, I rang Jo and told her she would have to take care of training for a few days. She completely understood – as I knew she would.

'Take all the time you need, Julie,' she said, and I could hear a wobble in her voice too. 'We're all going to really miss Pickles.'

Back at home I curled up under the duvet on the sofa with my remaining dogs, feeling a dreadful ache because Pickles wasn't curled in my lap. But, looking around at the dogs – who were all rescues – I realised they were Pickles's legacy. She had inspired me to keep my faith with rescue animals and proved that no matter how hard a start in life, with the right amount of love some dogs can do anything.

I knew that although Pickles was gone, she would stay in my heart for ever. Her fighting spirit, her quick mind and her incredibly loving heart. Yes, I was broken by her death, but I will always be so grateful for her extraordinary life.

Epilogue

There's just two weeks to go until Christmas and I have a rare afternoon off work. I'm so busy these days it feels as if Christmas has crept up on me without me even noticing. In fact, the whole year has flown by like a tornado.

It's several years since we lost Pickles, and Birds & Animals UK is the biggest company training animals for films in Britain. Sometimes it feels like I never get the chance to catch my breath, moving from project to project at breakneck speed and putting in gruelling hours on set. Directors have only got more demanding in recent years and we have to keep up, providing detailed updates during training time and completing endless paperwork before and after filming. I have a big team now, but even so I sometimes feel like I am being run ragged.

That's why I have to grab the days off when I can. I'm making the most of this one, having a Christmassy afternoon with my son, Luca, who is seven. We are wrapping presents beneath the twinkly tree lights, while the TV plays in the background. There's some silly festive film just coming to an end.

'Mummy, can you tie a bow on this one?' asks Luca, handing me a gift. I'm reaching for the ribbon when the TV announcer says something that makes me freeze.

'Coming up next, Colin Firth and Amanda Bynes star in the classic teen comedy *What a Girl Wants*.'

My heart is beating hard. I haven't watched the movie in years – in fact, I don't think I have seen it since it first came out. My instinct is to reach over and switch off the telly – it's just too painful to think of Pickles, even after all this time.

But then I hesitate. It would be wonderful to catch a glimpse of her again, wouldn't it?

As the opening credits roll, I pull Luca into a hug. 'This is one of Mummy's films,' I tell him. 'Pickles was in it. You were very little, but do you remember Pickles? How much you loved her?'

Luca was only three when Pickles died, but even then they had a special bond. He would pick her up like she was a cuddly toy and she would let him, without complaint, giving him the same devotion and love she gave to me.

'Yes, I remember Pickles! Let's watch it,' says Luca happily. Even at this age he's always saying he wants to be an animal trainer like me, so he loves to see the movies I've worked on.

We snuggle down on the sofa to watch the film, and I can feel a lump in my throat before Pickles has even appeared. But I'm determined to watch the film all the way through.

The moment Pickles bursts on screen, my heart leaps. There she is, my miracle puppy-farm dog! Her head cocked to the side in concentration, her eyes bright and her mouth parted as if she is smiling.

There are tears rolling silently down my face as I watch that garden party scene, memories crowding my head. I recall in excruciating detail my own hesitation and nervousness back then, when I was first striking out on my own. And I remember how Pickles had proved anything was possible, and that enormous emotional high when she delivered the perfect scene with so much joy.

As the film goes on, I barely pay attention to the story – in every scene she is in I am drawn to Pickles, seeing afresh how cute she is and trying to work out what she is thinking. In the scenes she's not in, I am simply waiting impatiently for her next appearance.

Why did it take me so long to watch this film? I wonder. It's like Pickles is alive again. I can almost feel her in the room.

'Mummy, why are you crying?' asks Luca, when the film finishes. Smiling, I wipe away my tears.

'I'm crying because I'm happy,' I tell him. 'Pickles was my best friend for a long time – and I haven't seen her for many years. It's very emotional for me to watch this film because she was such a special little dog.'

Luca considers this for a moment. 'What was so special about her?' he asks.

'Well, she was very brave,' I tell him, switching off the telly. 'And she was very loving. All of that was especially amazing because of where she came from . . .'

Luca is rapt as I tell him the story of little Pickles and her triumph over adversity. I tell him how I nursed her back to health and gave her a home, and how she in turn gave me courage, helped me make friends, saved a lost boy and got my new business off the ground. Mostly, I tell him how special she made me feel, and how you can never underestimate the love of a little animal.

Epilogue

As I talk, I wonder what Pickles would have made of all this. Instinctively, I know she would be pleased – she's the star of the show once more.

How to Spot a Puppy-Farm Dog

Pickles was lucky – animal welfare inspectors raided the puppy farm where she was suffering so terribly, and I was able to give her a loving new home. But many breeding bitches never get free of these hellholes.

As well as the horrors mother dogs are forced to endure, unscrupulous puppy farms are also breeding sick and dying puppies. Puppy farms across Europe are booming and many puppies are smuggled into the country from abroad. Often snatched from their mothers far too young, some puppies are trafficked hundreds of miles to be sold to unsuspecting owners. The evil breeders only stay in business because people keep buying their puppies, lining their pockets and keeping their immoral enterprises afloat.

But you can help by making sure you only buy a puppy bred in a safe and responsible environment, which will ensure both your pet and its mother have the best chance at a happy, healthy life.

Many puppy farmers advertise on the internet, and the RSPCA advises you read adverts carefully and look out for tell-tale signs. This is their advice on what to look out for:

- Dealers may use the same contact number on more than one advert. Try Googling the number to see if it has been used on any other puppy adverts.
- Descriptions may have been copied and pasted and used on more than one advert – try Googling the description and see if it has been used before, word for word.

WILL YOU TAKE ME HOME?

- Words like 'miniature' and 'teacup' can be a sign of dealers trying to capitalise on popular terms.
- Photos of the puppies may have been used on other adverts. Right-click on the photo, select 'search Google for image' and see if it has been used on other ads.
- If the advert says a puppy has been vaccinated, check how old he or she is. A puppy cannot be vaccinated before four to six weeks of age. So, if a person is advertising a three-week-old vaccinated puppy, they are lying.
- If the puppy is advertised as having a passport, it has most probably been imported.
- Some dealers claim they are Kennel Club Registered to convey legitimacy – but be wary of this, ask for original documents and check with the Kennel Club before buying a puppy.
- Promises of 'free insurance' and 'puppy

packs' do not mean the advert is from a legitimate breeder.

- If you see a suspicious advert, you can report it to the RSPCA so they can investigate by calling 0300 1234 999.

So how do you find a good puppy breeder instead? This is what the RSPCA says:

A responsible breeder will:

- Spend time chatting to you on the phone and will arrange a time for you to visit to meet their puppies, along with their mum and siblings, in the place where they were born and raised.
- Be happy to have more than one meeting to ensure you and the puppy are compatible.

- Be happy to answer all of your questions and ask you just as many to make sure their puppies are going to a good home.
- Be happy to show you their Local Authority licence if they are breeding and selling pets as a business (to make a profit).
- Provide genuine paperwork/certificates for puppy vaccinations, microchipping (which is a legal requirement), worming and results for health test where relevant.

A responsible breeder won't:

- Rush you into parting with cash in exchange for a puppy.
- Try to fob you off by saying that the mother is at the vet's, asleep or out for a walk. If mum isn't there, then the puppy wasn't bred there.
- Offer to deliver a puppy to you or meet you somewhere random like a car park.

- Say 'it's normal for the breed' about any health issues like snoring – all puppies should be born with the best chance of living happy, healthy lives, whatever breed they are.
- Use Kennel Club registration (or any other registration) as a guarantee of quality or health and happiness.

If anything seems suspicious, it means it is. Don't buy if you have any doubt in your mind.

I would also urge you to consider rescuing a dog if you can. There are thousands and thousands of dogs in rescue centres across the country who are desperate for a second chance at happiness in their forever home.

Giving them the love and care they deserve could be the most rewarding thing you ever do. It certainly has been for me.

Julie Tottman has been rescuing and training animals for the movies for over twenty-five years. Her credits include *Game of Thrones*, *Harry Potter* and *101 Dalmatians* among hundreds of others. She is a major advocate for animal welfare and feels very lucky to have her dream job.

The next book in the
Paws of Fame series

Coming February 2021